Excel

Magic

Tips & Time Savers

How to
increase your self-esteem
and worth to your company!

John H. Sweet

First Edition

Trafford Publishing   Cary Publishing, LLC

 www.trafford.com
North America & international
toll-free: 1 888 232 4444 (USA & Canada)
fax: 812 355 4082

To Kelley, Theresa and John

Acknowledgements

I have a number of people to thank for their help and support. My sincere thanks go to Kathy Caldwell, Maggie Wilson, Carol Golay Wantz and Dale Breedlove.

The entire team at Trafford Publishing deserves much of the credit for this book. Thank you Sarah Campbell for your friendly and professional help. You were a delight to work with.

Finally, thanks to my wife, my friend and my inspiration for over thirty years. Thanks Holly!

 JHS

Foreward

John Sweet is a master teacher, one of a kind – simply the best! It's the standard response from all of his students after completing John's courses.

I've had the good fortune of knowing and working with John over the last ten years, and he truly understands what is important when it comes to teaching computer software.

 "You don't know what you don't know", and John teaches, in a very professional way, what you need to know. He combines years of practical knowledge with delightful humor to create an atmosphere where users of all levels can relate and learn.

Part of John's success has come from his ability to make the difficult easy and to eliminate fear among his students, replacing it with an "I can" attitude! Watch the faces of his students when, for example, John teaches them how to create an Excel chart by pressing one key on the keyboard! Students light up with appreciation at the end of their courses with John!

I sincerely recommend this book to beginning and advanced users alike. I promise you will replace the old way of doing things (i.e. the long way or the wrong way) with hundreds of practical and useful shortcuts!

Kathy Caldwell
President
Knowledge Source Inc.

Preface – Note to the Reader

My sole criterion for the tips and time savers in this book was:

"How useful are they?"

I've taught public and corporate computer software classes for more than twelve years and have drawn from student feedback for this book. I know which tips and time savers make a lasting impression on people and which do not. The ones that do are in this book.

I always recommend taking the instructor-lead classes, but most people seem to reach a plateau after taking them. Frustration sets in. You ask yourself. Why am I so slow? Why do I have to ask someone for help? I know most of you won't go out and buy one of the very good, 50-pound books about Microsoft® Excel. Are they good? You bet. But I know that most corporate users of Excel don't buy them and won't read them.

This book will take you to the next level. I want you to be quicker and more comfortable with Excel. When you reach that next level, you will also feel better about yourself! My book is designed to increase your productivity and self-esteem. I hope it does both. If it does, then I've done my job.

This is not a reference book, but there is a detailed index, so you can research a situation.

You don't have to "read" this book from cover to cover, but I would recommend flipping through it page by page. The biggest problem with using today's software is, "You don't know what you don't know!" So – why don't you flip through the book – right now?

John H. Sweet

Contents

.

"Action is required to live the life you want to live."

—John H. Sweet: Author, Teacher and Publisher

1
Easy & Quick Tips

✓ Quick Chart
✓ Navigating Through Worksheets
✓ Close All
✓ Mouse Pointers Galore
✓ Clear Contents Vs. Delete
✓ Copying Formulas
✓ Looking at Large Lists
✓ Doing the Splits
✓ Easy Data Entry

"Making the simple complicated is commonplace; making the complicated simple, awesomely simple, that's creativity."

—*Charles Mingus*
legendary jazz musician

Page 18

Quick Chart

You need a chart in a hurry. Here's how to get it!

1.   Select the data you want to chart.

	A	B	C	D	E	F
1	Cary Publishing, LLC					
2						
3	Name	1st Qtr	2nd Qtr	3rd Qtr	4th Qtr	Yr Total
4	Long	110	175	140	168	$ 593
5	Olson	200	210	240	288	$ 938
6	Stark	300	180	295	354	$ 1,129
7	Unger	220	195	185	222	$ 822
8						

2.   Press the **F11** function key on your keyboard.

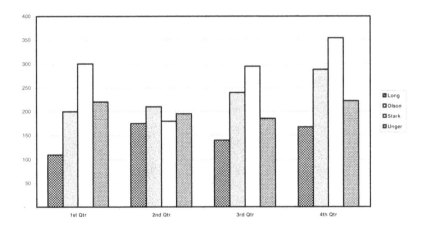

Bonus TIP!

If you want to go to the bottom or top of your **data**,

Press **CNTL + HOME**
or
Press **CNTL + END**

Please note that this will *not* take you to the end of the
worksheet, but only to the bottom of the data in the
worksheet.

PLUS: This also works in **MS Word**

Navigating through Worksheets

The following insert shows the scrolling buttons, the sheet tabs and the Horizontal scroll bar. The tab scrolling buttons allow you to move through the Sheet tabs when there are more tabs than will fit on the screen.

Click on the <u>inner</u> two scrolling buttons to move one sheet *without* changing the active sheet.

Clicking on the <u>outer</u> two buttons moves you to the first or last sheets.

You can also use the keyboard to navigate the sheet tabs.
Press **[CTRL+PageUp]** to move left one sheet.
Press **[CTRL+PageDown]** to move one sheet to the right.

Also, check this out!
Right click on any of the four arrows to bring up a menu showing the tab names. You can now navigate directly.

If there are more fifteen sheet tabs, you will have the choice of **More Sheets....**

Selecting **More Sheets...** brings up the *Activate* Dialog Box, which lists all of the sheet names. Selecting one navigates to it and makes it the active sheet.

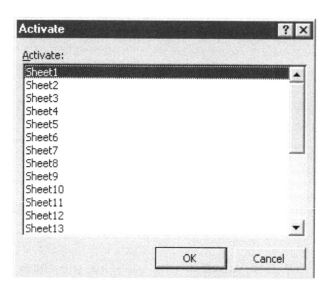

Bonus Tip

How big is a worksheet?

A worksheet is 16,777,216 cells – figure it out (256 x 65,536).

Now lets get a little more realistic. We usually have trouble visualizing 16 million anything!

Imagine the end zone of a football field. That's the size of your worksheet! WOW – that's big!

Close All

When you have a number of files open and you want to close them all.

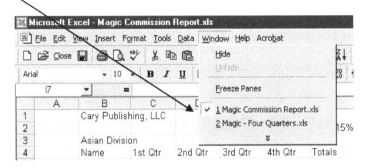

Don't take the time to shut them down one at a time.

Hold down your shift key while you click **File** on the menu bar. This dynamically changes the file menu from **Close** to **Close All**

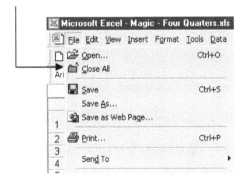

Note: You will still be asked if you want to keep any changes you've made.

Bonus Tip:

This works in **MS Word** as well!

More Close All:

If you want to use the keyboard to switch to **Close All**, Hold down **Shift** + **Alt** and press **F**. That will bring up the File menu with
Close All active.

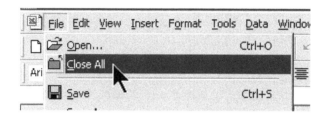

Notice the **C** in **Close All** is underlined. That means all you need to do to select it is enter the underlined letter, which in this case is a C. This will enter the **Close All** command.

Bonus Tip:

If you need a New Workbook
Press **Ctrl** + **N**

Mouse Pointers Galore

Excel has many different mouse pointers. So, here they are and how they work. Here they are and how they work.

The White Cross:	✛
Use the White Cross to ***Select*** cells and ranges of cells.	
The Arrow:	
Use the Arrow to *Move* and *Copy* cells and ranges. You ***Move*** with the arrow by clicking and dragging the mouse. You ***Copy*** by holding the **Ctrl** key down on the keyboard and then dragging the mouse. When you hold the **Ctrl** key down Excel places a small + sign on the mouse pointer indicating that you are Copying rather than Moving.	
The Cross Hair:	
Use the Cross Hair to reproduce the pattern you have selected. If you enter Jan in a cell and then drag the crosshair you will insert the Months of the year in the following sells. See the following.	

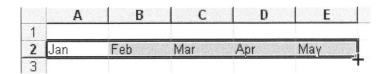

Books are the quietest and most constant of
Friends, the most accessible and wisest of
counselors, and the most patient of teachers."
—*Charles W. Eliot*

Clear Contents vs. Delete

Think of the cells of your worksheet as shoeboxes on edge. If you use the **Clear Contents** command you clean out the cell, but you don't change the structure of the worksheet. The shoeboxes are still there, but empty.

If you use the delete command you are actually changing the structure of the structure of the sheet. This is when you see this dialog box:

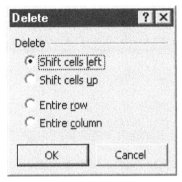

This is where you can get in real trouble!

The **Delete** Command **restructures** the worksheet. If you shift cells Left or Up you can destroy your spreadsheet. Be very careful when you use the **Delete** Command! Look at what happens to your sheet:

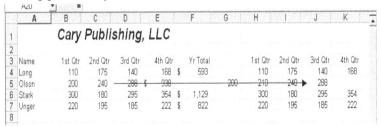

	Quiz: Which command do you execute when you press the Delete key on the keyboard?
	A. Delete
	B. Clear Contents
	C. Cross Out

Answer: B. Clear Contents

Is this confusing or what?

The **Delete** key issues the **Clear Contents** command – so be careful.

Urgent: Users new to Excel can cause major problems with existing worksheets by using **Delete** when instead of **Clear Contents**.

Copying Formulas

The fill handle is the black box in the lower right hand corner of the cell or range. If you place the mouse pointer over the Fill Handle it will turn into a Cross Hair. You can click and hold the Cross Hair and drag down to copy the formula.

F4	▼	=	=SUM(B4:E4)		
	A	B	C	D	E	F

	A	B	C	D	E	F
1	*Cary Publishing, LLC*					
2						
3	Name	1st Qtr	2nd Qtr	3rd Qtr	4th Qtr	Yr Total
4	Urmston	110	175	140	168	$ 593
5	Lingle	200	210	240	288	
6	Golay	300	180	295	354	
7	Corsi	220	195	185	222	

This is fine when you only have to copy a few rows, but if you happen to have more than a few rows, dragging is very awkward.

If you want to copy the formula down all the way, place your mouse pointer on the Fill Handle to get the Cross Hair, then double click.

Excel fills in the formula for all the following rows.

F4	▼	=	=SUM(B4:E4)		

	A	B	C	D	E	F
1	*Cary Publishing, LLC*					
2						
3	Name	1st Qtr	2nd Qtr	3rd Qtr	4th Qtr	Yr Total
4	Urmston	110	175	140	168	$ 593
5	Lingle	200	210	240	288	
6	Golay	300	180	295	354	
7	Corsi	220	195	185	222	

F4			=	=SUM(B4:E4)		

	A	B		D	E	F
1		*Cary Publishing, LLC*				
2						
3	Name	1st Qtr	2nd Qtr	3rd Qtr	4th Qtr	Yr Total
4	Urmston	110	175	140	168	$ 593
5	Lingle	200	210	240	288	$ 938
6	Golay	300	180	295	354	$ 1,129
7	Corsi	220	195	185	222	$ 822
8						

(Formula Bar)

This is a real time saver.

Looking at Long Lists

When looking at a long list of data, how do you keep the heading on the screen? The solution is easy.

1. Click in a cell immediately under the row that contains the column headings.
2. Select **Window** from the Menu bar and click **Freeze Panes**.

Now you can scroll the data up and down as well as horizontally and still see the Headings.

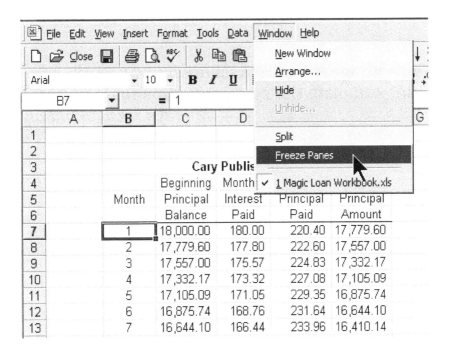

When you are finished, select Windows again and click on Unfreeze Panes.

Indeed one feels like a failure if one's work does
not stimulate the next generation to do better.

—*Mihaly Csikszentmihalyi*

Doing The Splits

You can split your screen by using the **Window/Split** command on the Menu bar, or as a quick alternative, using the mouse like this:

1.   Locate the small rectangle at the very end of either scroll bar and move your mouse pointer over it. Your pointer will turn into a double line double arrow.

2.   You can then click and drag it down or over. Your screen will split horizontally where you release the placeholder.

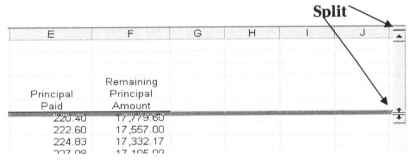

Split

E	F	G	H	I	J
Principal Paid	Remaining Principal Amount				
220.40	17,779.60				
222.60	17,557.00				
224.83	17,332.17				
227.08	17,105.09				

3.   When you split the screen with both the horizontal and vertical scroll bars, you will be able to scroll information in two dimensions.

Two Splits

	A	B	F
1			
2			
3			
4			Remaining
5		Month	Principal
6			Amount
7		1	177,796.00
8		2	175,569.96
9		3	173,321.66
10		4	171,050.87

"Unfortunate the master who has no apprentices to surpass him."

—*Leonardo da Vinci*

Easy Data Entry

Here's how to simplify entering data.

1. Select the area where you plan to enter data.
2. Enter the first data and press Enter. Enter moves the selection down a cell and is ready to accept the next data. When you are at the bottom of the column and press Enter, you jump to the top of the next selected column.

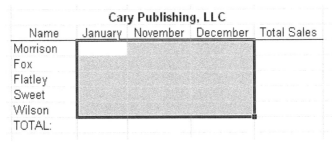

If you want to move horizontally rather than vertically when you press the enter key go to:

1. **Tools/Options** then select the **Edit** tab. You can then change the "Move selection after Enter Direction" combination box.

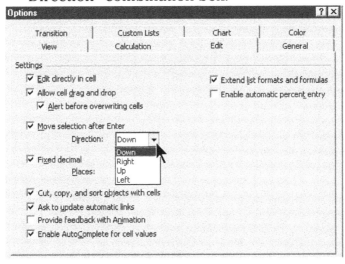

"Practice yourself in little things, and thence proceed to greater."

—*Epictetus*

2
Goodies Galore

- ✓ Name that cell
- ✓ Range Names
- ✓ Answers in a hurry
- ✓ Best Fit
- ✓ Absolute References
- ✓ Custom Lists
- ✓ Fill Series

"Do you want to be the statue or the bird?"
—*Francis Weaver*

Name That Cell

What's easier to remember FS3356 or FirstQtr?

Of course FirstQtr is. Well then, why don't you name the cell or range FirstQtr? It will also make more sense when used in a formula!

Here is a quick way to give a cell a name:

1.   Select the cell or range.
2.   ┌Click in the **Name Box**, which is located on the far left end of the **Equation Bar**. Make sure you click <u>between</u> the address and the arrow for the combination box. Don't click on the Arrow by mistake.
3.   │ Type the name your want (No Spaces Allowed)
4.   └ Press the **Enter** key.

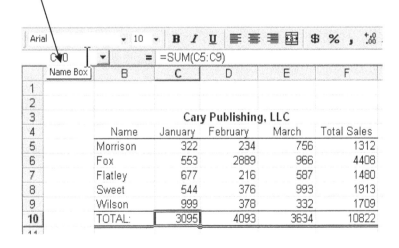

The cell or range can now be referenced by the name you gave it!!

Let's say the going commission rate is 15%, and you want to assign the value 15% to the name "Comm". Then you can use Comm in formulas. If the commission percentage changes all you have to do is change the value assigned to the name Comm.

Here's how to assign a "value" to a Name:

1. Select Insert/Name/Define Name.
2. Type the name in the Names in Workbook: field.
3. Type your value in the Refers to: field.
4. Click Add/OK.

Now any time you type Comm it will refer to 15%.

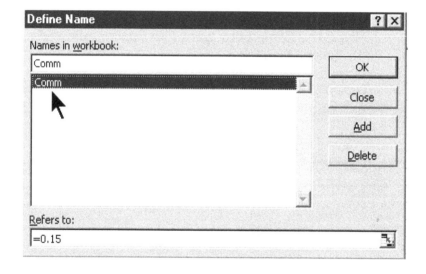

Now that's another time saver!

Range Names

You can create range names quickly from existing headings.

In this example we will use the Row headings to name the ranges. You can also use the Column Heading.

1. Select the Row heading and ranges you want to name.

	A	B	C	D	E	F
1		Cary Publishing, LLC				
2	NC Division					
3	Name	1st Qtr	2nd Qtr	3rd Qtr	4th Qtr	Totals
4	Lingle	125	443	453	750	1771
5	Fox	206	210	326	475	1217
6	Morrison	308	180	395	100	983
7	Toms	250	200	166	588	1204
8	Knight	720	195	335	664	1914
9	TOTAL:	1609	1228	1675	2577	7089

2. Select **Insert/Name/Create**.

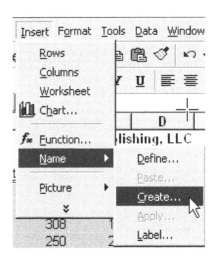

3. Select **Left Column** from the Create Names dialog box.
4. Click **OK**

5. Select the Name Box to see the Names and named ranges

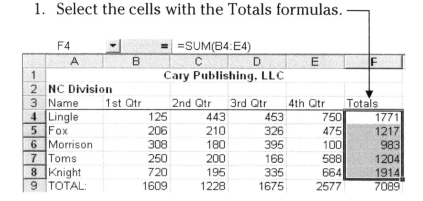

Now lets include the Names in the formulas in column F.

1. Select the cells with the Totals formulas.

	A	B	C	D	E	F
1			Cary Publishing, LLC			
2	NC Division					
3	Name	1st Qtr	2nd Qtr	3rd Qtr	4th Qtr	Totals
4	Lingle	125	443	453	750	1771
5	Fox	206	210	326	475	1217
6	Morrison	308	180	395	100	983
7	Toms	250	200	166	588	1204
8	Knight	720	195	335	664	1914
9	TOTAL:	1609	1228	1675	2577	7089

2. Select **Insert/Name/Apply**.

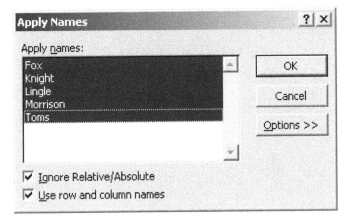

3. Click **OK**.

Notice the formulas after I entered **CTRL** + ` (The leftmost key on the top row of the keyboard).

	F4			=	=SUM(Lingle)	
	A	B	C	D	E	F
1				Cary Publishing, LLC		
2	NC Division					
3	Name	1st Qtr	2nd Qtr	3rd Qtr	4th Qtr	Totals
4	Lingle	125	443	453	750	=SUM(Lingle)
5	Fox	206	210	326	475	=SUM(Fox)
6	Morrison	308	180	395	100	=SUM(Morrison)
7	Toms	250	200	166	588	=SUM(Toms)
8	Knight	720	195	335	664	=SUM(Knight)
9	TOTAL:	=SUM(B4:B8)	=SUM(C4:C8)	=SUM(D4:D8)	=SUM(E4:E8)	=SUM(F4:F8)

Here is the standard view.

	F4			=	=SUM(Lingle)	
	A	B	C	D	E	F
1				Cary Publishing, LLC		
2	NC Division					
3	Name	1st Qtr	2nd Qtr	3rd Qtr	4th Qtr	Totals
4	Lingle	125	443	453	750	1771
5	Fox	206	210	326	475	1217
6	Morrison	308	180	395	100	983
7	Toms	250	200	166	588	1204
8	Knight	720	195	335	664	1914
9	TOTAL:	1609	1228	1675	2577	7089

"Successful people work to discover their talents, to develop those talents, and then to use those talents to benefit others as well as themselves."
—*Tom Morris*
Author and Speaker

Remembering Cell Names

If you have forgotten the cell or range name you need to place in a formula, or you don't want to type it:

1. Complete your formula up to the point that you need to enter the cell or range name.
2. Press F3 to display the range names.
3. Double click on the name you need to insert into your formula.

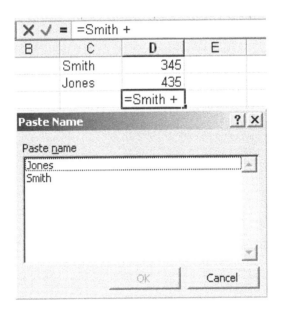

"Shoulda, coulda, and woulda won't get it done. In attacking adversity, only a positive attitude, alertness, and regrouping to basics can launch a comeback."

—Pat Riley
Legendary Basketball Coach

Answers in a Hurry!

Your boss wants to know how much of the principal the company paid in the first year of a loan. Use the AutoCalculate feature to get the answer in a hurry!

1. Select the numbers you want to add.
2. Look down in the lower right hand corner of the worksheet and there is your answer.

Hey, that's fast!

Interest Paid	Principal Paid	Remaining Principal Amount
180.00	220.40	17,779.60
177.80	222.60	17,557.00
175.57	224.83	17,332.17
173.32	227.08	17,105.09
171.05	229.35	16,875.74
168.76	231.64	16,644.10
166.44	233.96	16,410.14
164.10	236.30	16,173.84
161.74	238.66	15,935.18
159.35	241.05	15,694.13
156.94	243.46	15,450.67
154.51	245.89	15,204.78
152.05	248.35	14,956.42
149.56	250.84	14,705.59
147.06	253.34	14,452.24
144.52	255.88	14,196.37
141.96	258.44	13,937.93

heet / Sheet3 /

Sum=2,795.22

You want more answers – Right Click on the answer (Sum=2,795.22) and get this:

Now you can get the Average, Count, Max and other answers.

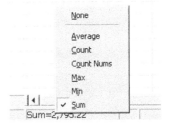

None
Average
Count
Count Nums
Max
Min
✓ Sum
Sum=2,795.22

Bonus TIP!

Want to Time or Date Stamp a cell?

Here's how:

1. **Select** your cell.
2. For a <u>Date Stamp</u> hold down the **Control** key and press the semi-colon: **CNTL + ;**
3. For a <u>Time Stamp</u> hold down both the **Control** and the **Shift** keys then press the colon: **CNTL + Shift + :**

	A	B	C
1	CNTL + ; ⟶		04/03/2002
2			
3	CNTL + SHIFT + : ⟶		3:50 PM

Best Fit

If you want to make sure a column is as wide as the widest item in the column, use Best Fit. You can Best Fit one column or multiple columns at a time.

You could simply drag the column to make it wider or narrower, but when you do it this way you can't see the data below your screen, so you can't tell how wide to make the column.

Simply place your insertion point between two columns until you see the double arrow and double click.

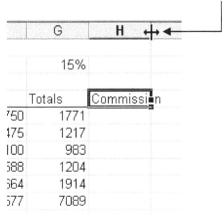

If you are doing multiple columns, select them all, move the mouse pointer to the right most column selected and then double click the mouse pointer.

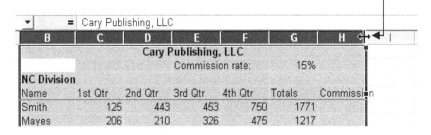

"Big shots are only little shots who keep shooting."

—*Christopher Morley*

Absolute References

If you don't want to let part or all of a formula to change when copying the formula to another address, you need to use an Absolute Reference. Simply insert dollar signs in front of the part of the formula you want to make absolute.

For an example if you have the following as your formula, =G5*G2 and want to make the G3 portion absolute, you would change the formula to =G5*G2.

A shortcut here is to place the insertion point between the G and the 2 in the equation bar and press F4 on your keyboard. Excel will then put the dollar signs in for you.

▼	=	=G5*G2					
B	C	D	E	F	G	H	
			Cary Publishing, LLC				
			Commission rate:		15%		
NC Division							
Name	1st Qtr	2nd Qtr	3rd Qtr	4th Qtr	Totals	Commission	
Lingle	125	443	453	750	1771	265.65	
Fox	206	210	326	475	1217	182.55	
Morrison	308	180	395	100	983	147.45	
Toms	250	200	166	588	1204	180.6	
Knight	720	195	335	664	1914	287.1	
TOTAL:	1609	1228	1675	2577	7089	1063.35	

Now when you copy the formula from H5 through H10 the Commission rate field stays at G2 and gives you the correct commission rate.

"Failure is an event, never a person; an attitude, not an outcome."

—*Zig Ziglar*

Custom Lists

Custom Lists are great time savers for people who work with lists, which is about everyone. You can create a custom list and use it whenever you need it.

Here are the steps to creating a custom list:

1. Create your list.
2. Select your list
3. Go to **Tools/Options**
4. Select the **Custom Lists** tab
5. **Click Import**
6. Click **OK**

The list you just created will be available until you delete it.

When you are ready to use the list simply type one of the items on the list. Move your mouse pointer over the **Fill Handle** (the black box at the lower right hand corner of your selected cell) and it will turn into a black cross hair. Then click and drag to display the list.

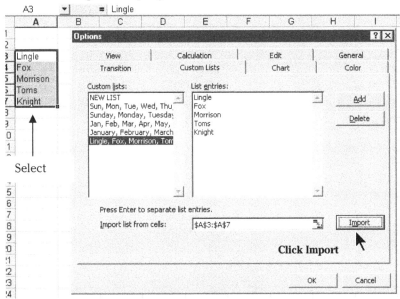

You can also **Sort** by your custom list!

1   Click on **Data/Sort**.
2   Click on the **Options** button.
3   Click on the arrow for the **First Key Sort Order**.

Now you will see where you can select your **Custom List** and use it for the sort order.

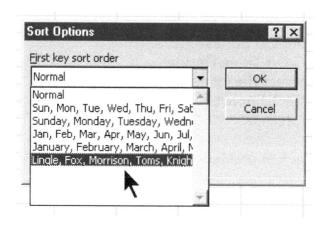

Fill Series

Excel will expand any pattern you give it. Let's start with the months of the year:

You type January in a cell. Then select the Fill Handle at the bottom right of the cell with the black cross hair.

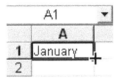

Drag it down or over.

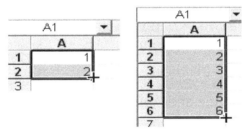

If you want to get 1,2,3,4,etc. you have to give it a pattern of 1 and 2.

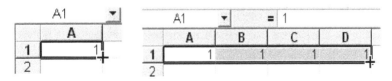

Caution: A common mistake is having just a single cell pattern.

Note: If you have a single entry, hold the **CTRL** key down when you drag the Fill Handle to get 1,2,3...

Let's look at one more pattern.

Here we have selected a two-cell range.

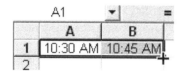

When we reproduce the pattern we get this.

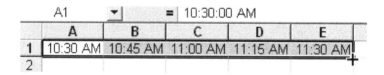

Urgent

There are two very common mistakes made here.

1. One is leaving the space out between the time and AM.

2. The second mistake is more common. Many people want to put periods after the A and the M like this A.M. which is incorrect and will cause Excel to treat it as text rather than time.

3
Fun Tips

- ✓ Fonts are Fun
- ✓ Rotate
- ✓ Magic Feature
- ✓ Too Many Pages
- ✓ Default Font
- ✓ Quick Max

"Decisions determine destiny."
—*Fredrick Speakman*

Fonts are Fun

Did you learn to type in school? I mean real typing on a typewriter, not keyboarding on a computer. Here's a test question for you typewriter students.

> On a typewriter how much smaller
> was a lower case i letter than a

Answer:

> Each letter was the same size. Therefore we could easily measure the type by the number of characters per inch!

When computers were designed we started using variable fonts. The actual characters are different sizes depending which characters you select. Now the fonts are measured in Points, which is a printing term. Since most of us aren't printers, there is only one rule you need to know and it is:

There are 72 Points
in
1 Inch!

"…only *applied* knowledge is power."
—Brian Tracey

Rotate

You can rotate the headings to reduce the width of the column when the column headings are wider than the data in the columns.

1. Select the cells you want to rotate.
2. Select **Format/Cells** and the **Alignment** tab.
3. Under Orientation on the right side of the Dialog box, click on the red diamond and drag it Up or Down 45°.
4. Click **OK**.

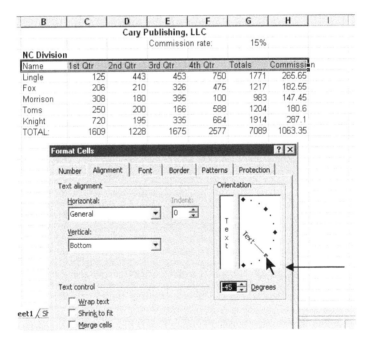

This allows you to change the degree of rotation. The result is on the next page.

The result!

B	C	D	E	F	G	H
		Cary Publishing, LLC				
			Commission rate:		15%	
NC Division						
Name	*1st Qtr*	*2nd Qtr*	*3rd Qtr*	*4th Qtr*	*Totals*	*Commission*
Lingle	125	443	453	750	1771	265.65
Fox	206	210	326	475	1217	182.55

Now you can reduce the size of the columns as necessary.

Magic Feature

If you are prone to typos—the **AutoCorrect** feature is for you

When you type a word like **teh** in a cell and hit the space bar   **AutoCorrect** compares the word you typed to the "Replace:" list in its dialog box. And if it finds a match, substitutes the word in the "With:" column.

Select **Tools/AutoCorrect**

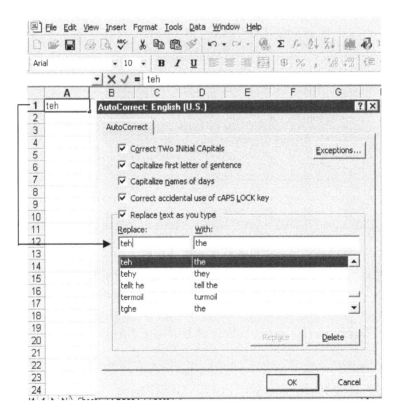

When you type a word and hit the space bar, **AutoCorrect** searches through the **Replace** Column and if it finds a match, substitutes the word in the width column.

Helping the AutoCorrect System

If you have a long company name
such as International Business
Machines

Try typing
ibm-
in the "Replace:" cell
and
International Business Machines
in the "With:" cell.

Now when you type ibm- and press
the space bar it will insert
International Business Machines

Bonus Tip

You can add to **AutoCorrect** from **Spell Check**.
When **Spell Check** finds a misspelled word,
click on the **AutoCorrect** button. **Spell Check**
automatically inserts the misspelled word and
the correct word into **AutoCorrect**, so it can
correct the misspelling in the future.

Too Many Pages

You print the report for your boss and it's just a little more that one page. You know what he's going to say, "Can't you get this to on one page?"

This Column won't fit here

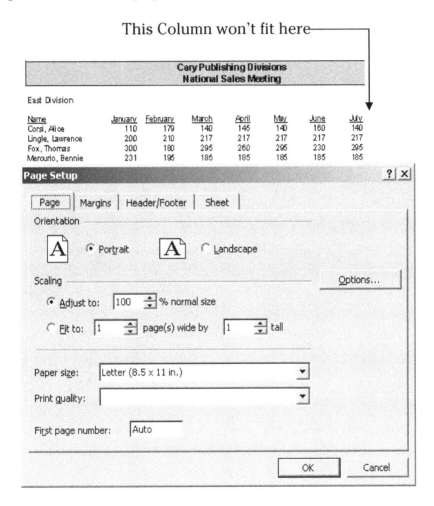

The document doesn't fit so – (*Next Page*)

Change the Scaling like this:

1. Select **Print Preview**.
2. Click the Setup button.
3. Under Scaling, Select **Fit to**:
4. Change Pages to 1 by 1.
5. Click **OK**

Now it fits on one page!

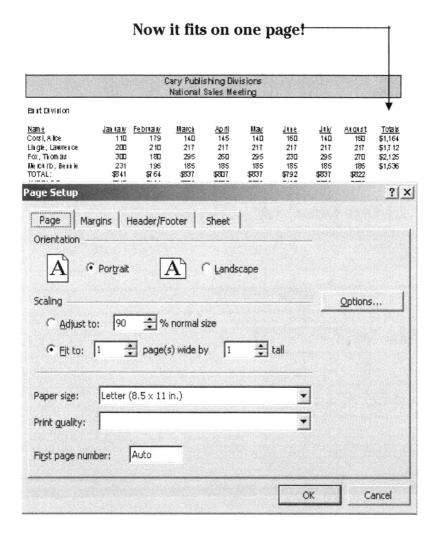

Default Font

How do you set the default font so that all of the books you create have this font?

1. Select **Tools/Options**.
2. Select the **General** tab.
3. In the Standard font box select a **Font**.
4. In the Size box select a Size.

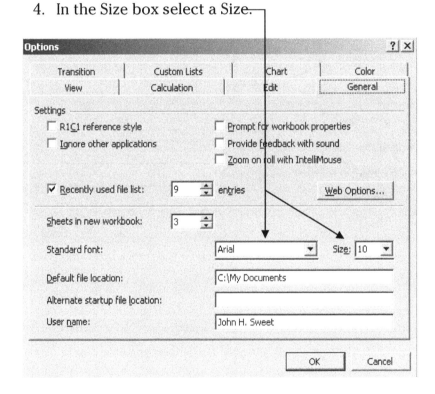

You have to restart Microsoft® Excel before the defaults will be used for new workbooks. Existing workbooks are not changed.

Additional Settings in the **General** tab:

You also set the number of **Sheets** in a new workbook and the number of entries in the recently used file list, which is the last thing in the **File** menu.

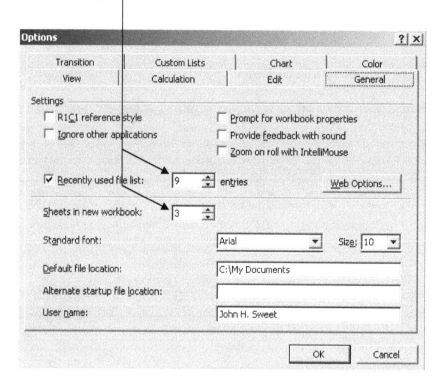

Quick Max

I know – your trifocals get in the way when you try to click that little **Maximize** tool in the upper right hand corner to the window.

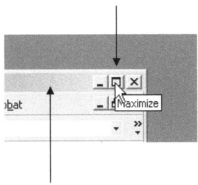

These tools are hard to see for some of us with "aging" eyes. Instead just double click on the blue title bar to **Maximize** your windows.

When you double click the title bar in a maximized window it will **Restore** it.

"A goal without an action plan is a daydream."
—Dr. Nathaniel Branden

Rapid Data Entry

If you want the same entry to appear in a number of cells, you can enter all of them in one process. The entry can be text, a value or a formula.

1. Select the range you want the same entry to appear in.

2. Type the entry in the first cell.

3. Select CTRL + Enter.

"An Investment in knowledge pays the best
interest."

—Benjamin Franklin

4
Good Stuff

- ✓ Three-D References
- ✓ Great Views
- ✓ Formula Viewing
- ✓ On the Internet
- ✓ Remember Your Workspace
- ✓ Rapid Data Entry

"If one advances confidently in the direction of his dreams and endeavors to live the life he has imagined, he will meet with a success unexpected in common hours."

—Henry David Thoreau

Three-D References

Summarizing data from different sheets in a workbook is called
Three Dimensional Referencing.
In this example we are using five sheets. We want to add the figures from the Indiana Sheet through the Texas Sheet and place the answer on the Summary Sheet.

1. You always start in the cell where you want the answer. Click in B4 on the Summary Sheet and Type =**Sum(**

Item	QTR 1	QTR 2	QTR 3	QTR 4
Hardware	=Sum(			
Software				
Equipment				
Misc.				
Totals:	$0	$0	$0	$0

Indiana / Colorado / North Carolina / Texas \ **Summary**

2. Then select the Indiana Sheet and B4.

SUM		✗ ✓ =	=Sum(Indiana!B4	
	A	B	C	D	E

	A	B	C	D	E
1	Indiana Division				
2					
3	Item	QTR 1	QTR 2	QTR 3	QTR 4
4	Hardware	320	800	1000	500
5	Software	400	90	800	200
6	Equipment	250	500	500	200
7	Misc.	200	431	600	300
8	Totals:	$1,170	$1,821	$2,900	$1,200

3. Hold your **Shift** key down and click on the Texas Sheet. You will notice all of the sheets are selected.

\ **Indiana** / Colorado / North Carolina / Texas / Summary /

4. Next press your **ENTER** key. You will now have the 3-D answer in cell B4 in your Summary Sheet!

5. **Notice** the formula: =Sum(Indiana:Texas!B4). Learn to read formulas from right to left. This is a Sum function, now reading from right to left you see that we are going to sum B4 in the

B4	▼	=	=SUM(Indiana:Texas!B4)		
	A	B	C	D	E
1	Summary				
2					
3	Item	QTR 1	QTR 2	QTR 3	QTR 4
4	Hardware	1020			
5	Software				
6	Equipment				
7	Misc.				
8	Totals:	$1,020	$0	$0	$0

Range of Sheets from Indiana through Texas!

6. Now place your mouse on the Fill Handle (the black box in the lower right corner of cell B4) and drag three cells to the right.

B4	▼	=	=SUM(Indiana:Texas!B4)		
	A	B	C	D	E
1	Summary				
2					
3	Item	QTR 1	QTR 2	QTR 3	QTR 4
4	Hardware	1020	2700	3300	1600
5	Software				
6	Equipment				
7	Misc.				
8	Totals:	$1,020	$2,700	$3,300	$1,600

Wow, this isn't tough – keep going!

7. Double Click the crosshair and you will complete the
    3-D calculations for your workbook!

	A	B	C	D	E
1	Summary				
2					
3	Item	QTR 1	QTR 2	QTR 3	QTR 4
4	Hardware	1020	2700	3300	1600
5	Software	1100	1390	2700	1200
6	Equipment	950	1800	2900	900
7	Misc.	900	1331	1400	900
8	Totals:	$3,970	$7,221	$10,300	$4,600

Note: The Techies of the world refer to the Exclamation point (!) in a formula as a **Bang**!

=SUM(Indiana:Texas!C7)

"He who walks in the middle of the road gets hit from both sides."

—*George P. Schultz*

Great Views

You can save the current view so you can come back to it. It saves the settings and allows you to return whenever you like.

We will start with this worksheet.

	A	B	C	D	E	F
1	Cary Publishing, LLC					
2						
3	Name	1st Qtr	2nd Qtr	3rd Qtr	4th Qtr	Yr Total
4	Urmston	110	175	140	168	$ 593
5	Lingle	200	210	240	288	$ 938
6	Golay	300	180	295	354	$ 1,129
7	Corsi	220	195	185	222	$ 822

Now, hide the columns.
1. Select columns C and D
2. Right click on the selected area
3. Choose **Hide**.

	A	B	E	F
1	Cary Publishing, LLC			
2				
3	Name	1st Qtr	4th Qtr	Yr Total
4	Urmston	110	168	$ 593
5	Lingle	200	288	$ 938
6	Golay	300	354	$ 1,129
7	Corsi	220	222	$ 822

Now save the view.

1. Click **View** on the Menu Bar
2. Select **Custom Views...**

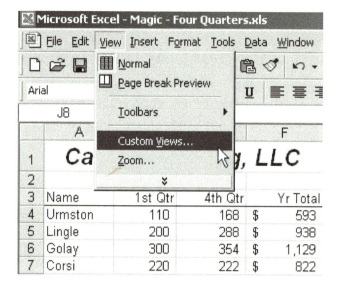

That brings up the **Custom Views** Dialog box.

Click **Add...** and name your view. I'll name it
FirstAndFourthQuarters.

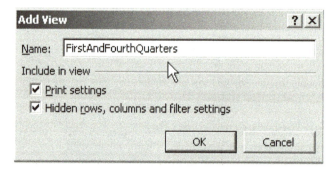

Whenever you want to return to the view
FirstAndFourthQuarters,

Select:

1. **View**
2. **Custom Views**
3. **FirstAndFourthQuarters**
4. **Show**

"Everything comes to him who hustles while he waits."

—*Thomas Edison*

Formula Viewing

Do you need to see all of your worksheet's formulas so you can check them or even print them out?

Here is our worksheet.

	A	B	C	D	E	F
1						
2		Cary Publishing, LLC				
3		Quarterly Sales Report				
4						
5	Location	Qtr 1	Qtr 2	Qtr 3	Qtr 4	Total
6	Australia	$1,550.00	$1,600.00	$3,100.00	$4,400.00	$10,650.00
7	Canada	1,525.00	1,900.00	2,500.00	4,900.00	10,825.00
8	Great Britain	1,200.00	1,500.00	1,400.00	5,400.00	9,500.00
9	USA	1,700.00	1,840.00	1,625.00	2,800.00	7,965.00
10	Quarter Total	$5,975.00	$6,840.00	$8,625.00	$17,500.00	$38,940.00
11						

To see the formulas:

1. Press CTRL + ` (The leftmost key on your keyboard's top row.)

	Cary Publishing, LLC				
	Quarterly Sales Report				
Location	Qtr 1	Qtr 2	Qtr 3	Qtr 4	Total
Australia	1550	1600	3100	4400	=SUM(B6:E6)
Canada	1525	1900	2500	4900	=SUM(B7:E7)
Great Britain	1200	1500	1400	5400	=SUM(B8:E8)
USA	1700	1840	1625	2800	=SUM(B9:E9)
Quarter Total	=SUM(B6:B9)	=SUM(C6:C9)	=SUM(D6:D9)	=SUM(E6:E9)	=SUM(F6:F9)

To restore the view and column widths:

2. Press CTRL + ` again!

Neat Tip!

Bonus Tip

Formula Errors

If you have a long formula with an error in it and are having trouble locating the error, try this.

Convert the formula to text by removing the = that starts the formula. Now Excel will allow you to move on and trouble shoot the error later.

When you think you have the error corrected, insert the = sign again converting the text back to a formula.

On the Internet

Microsoft® has made it easy to save files for use on the Internet or your Intranet.

All you have to do is:

1. Select **File** then
2. **Save as Web Page...**

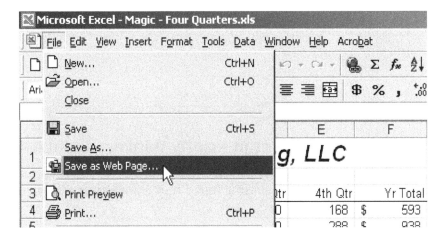

Your file will be saved in HTML (Hyper Text Mark Up) language to whatever location you select.

"No one learns his craft just by thinking about it. It must be practiced.

—*Rachel Vater*

Remember Your Workspace

Saving a workspace means you save all of the Excel files you have open, with the view you have selected and the position they're in when you saved the workspace.

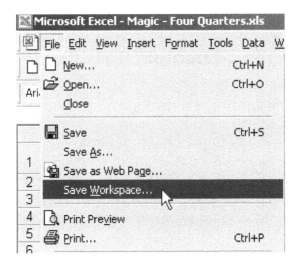

Give the Workspace a name and save it wherever you want.

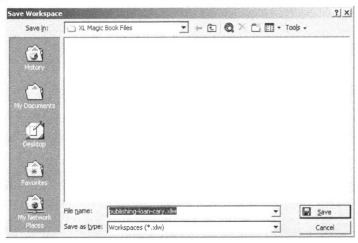

When you want to bring the Workspace back up, simply open it. It will open any files and position them the way they were when you saved the workspace.

The Workspace files have an **.xlw** extension and can be sent to someone else, but you must also send the original Excel (**.xls**) files!

Bonus TIP!

If you want to cycle through open Workbooks
and other running programs such as
MS Word or **MS Outlook**...

Press:
Alt + Tab + Tab + Tab...
until you get to the screen you need.

5
Quick Navigation

✓ Move to Open Workbooks
✓ Go to a cell
✓ Quick Worksheet Movement
✓ Move or Copy a Worksheet
✓ Outlining

"The future belongs to the competent."
—*Brian Tracy*

Move to Open Workbooks

You can use the **Windows** command in the **Menu** bar to move to other **Workbooks**,

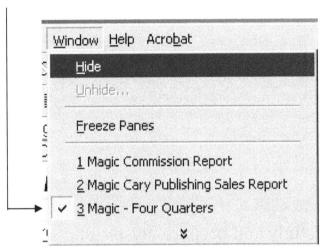

or

You can click on your selection in the taskbar,

or

Cycle through the open workbooks by

Pressing **Ctrl + F6 + F6 +**

Bonus:
1. To show the worksheets in the task bar:
2. Select **Tools/Options/View**
3. Check **Windows In Taskbar**.

"I will study and prepare myself, and someday my chance will come."

—*Abraham Lincoln*

Going to a Cell

Navigating to a cell is easy.

1. Press **Ctrl + G** or **F5**

2. Type the address you want to go to and press **OK**.

If you bring the **Go To** dialog box up again, it will have the cell you left as the current reference so you can return to it.

"More gold has been mined from the thoughts of men than has ever been taken from the earth."

—*Napoleon Hill*

Quick Sheet Movement

To move to the next worksheet:

Press **Ctrl** + **Page Down**

Of course

Ctrl + **Page Up**

will take you to the previous worksheet!

Bonus TIP!

Giant Worksheet Scrolling

If you need to scroll in a very large worksheet,

Press **Shift** while you drag either scroll box.

"You can tell how high you will rise in life by how deeply you dig your foundation of practical knowledge and skill."

—Brian Tracey

Move or Copy a Worksheet

To **Move** a sheet you can drag the sheet along the row of worksheet tabs. Notice the down pointing arrow as a placeholder.

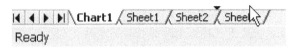

To **Copy** a sheet hold the **Ctrl** key down while dragging.

> **Note**: If you select several tabs with Ctrl + click before you drag to move or copy, this will move or copy all of them!

Want to *Move* a worksheet to another workbook:

Open both workbooks
Select Window/Arrange...

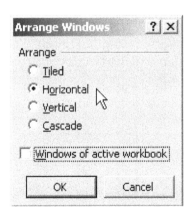

Select Horizontal
Click OK

You *Move* the sheet if you drag a sheet tab from one workbook to another. You *Copy* the sheet if you hold the **Ctrl** key down when you drag it.

Magic - Four Quarters.xls

	A	B	C	D	E	F
1			Cary Publishing, LLC			
2						
3	Name	1st Qtr	2nd Qtr	3rd Qtr	4th Qtr	Yr Total
4	Urmston	110	175	140	168	$ 593
5	Lingle	200	210	240	288	$ 938
6	Golay	300	180	295	354	$ 1,129
7	Corsi	220	195	185	222	$ 822
8						
9						
10						
11						
12						
13						

Chart1 \ **Cary Publishing, LLC** / Sheet2 / Sheet3 /

Magic - Small Sort.xls

	A	B	C	D	E	F
1			Cary Publishing, LLC			
2						
3	Name	1st Qtr	2nd Qtr	3rd Qtr	4th Qtr	Yr Total
4	Urmston	110	175	140	168	$ 593
5	Lingle	200	210	240	288	$ 938
6	Golay	300	180	295	354	$ 1,129
7	Corsi	220	195	185	222	$ 822
8						
9						
10						
11						
12						
13						

Small Sort \ **Cary Publishing, LLC** / Sheet2 / Sheet3 /

Outlining

You can have nine levels of outlining! This is neat stuff!

You start with your data. For example, use four quarters displayed in columns like this. Notice that column E and I have formulas in them as well as rows 7, 12 and 14. Outlining keys on the cells that contain formulas – so be consistent with their placement.

	A	B	C	D	E	F	G	H	I
					Qtr 1				Qtr 2
1		Jan	Feb	Mar	Total	Apr	May	June	Total
2	Sales								
3									
4	Apples	110	165	165	$440	200	175	200	$575
5	Peaches	165	200	250	$615	250	200	175	$625
6	Pears	110	175	200	$485	200	225	165	$590
7	Total Fruit	$385	$540	$615	$1,540	$650	$600	$540	$1,790
8									
9	Beans	325	350	275	$950	325	325	325	$975
10	Corn	325	325	250	$900	250	200	250	$700
11	Lettuce	250	325	275	$850	200	250	225	$675
12	Total Vegetables	$900	$1,000	$800	$2,700	$775	$775	$800	$2,350
13									
14	Total Sales	$1,285	$1,540	$1,415	$4,240	$1,425	$1,375	$1,340	$4,140

Select **Data/Group and Outline/Auto Outline**.

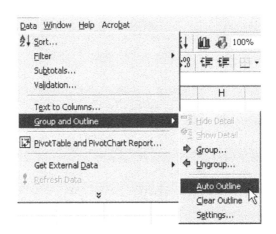

The result looks like this with vertical and horizontal numbers located on the top left of the data.

	A	B	C	D	E	F	G	H	I
					Qtr 1				Qtr 2
1		Jan	Feb	Mar	Total	Apr	May	June	Total
2	Sales								
3									
4	Apples	110	165	165	$440	200	175	200	$575
5	Peaches	165	200	250	$615	250	200	175	$625
6	Pears	110	175	200	$485	200	225	165	$590
7	Total Fruit	$385	$540	$615	$1,540	$650	$600	$540	$1,790
8									
9	Beans	325	350	275	$950	325	325	325	$975
10	Corn	325	325	250	$900	250	200	250	$700
11	Lettuce	250	325	275	$850	200	250	225	$675
12	Total Vegetables	$900	$1,000	$800	$2,700	$775	$775	$800	$2,350
13									
14	Total Sales	$1,285	$1,540	$1,415	$4,240	$1,425	$1,375	$1,340	$4,140

When you click on the numbers you get different displays of the data. Here I clicked on the 2 in the vertical row. Cool!

	A	E	I	M	Q	R
		Qtr 1	Qtr 2	Qtr3	Qtr4	Annual
1		Total	Total	Total	Total	Totals
2	Sales					
3						
4	Apples	$440	$575	$675	$850	$2,540
5	Peaches	$615	$625	$825	$715	$2,780
6	Pears	$485	$590	$640	$775	$2,490
7	Total Fruit	$1,540	$1,790	$2,140	$2,340	$7,810
8						
9	Beans	$950	$975	$800	$775	$3,500
10	Corn	$900	$700	$825	$975	$3,400
11	Lettuce	$850	$675	$925	$825	$3,275
12	Total Vegetables	$2,700	$2,350	$2,550	$2,575	$10,175
13						
14	Total Sales	$4,240	$4,140	$4,690	$4,915	$17,985

6
Quick Create/Delete

✓ New Workbook
✓ Closing a Workbook
✓ Quick New Worksheet
✓ Easy Sheet Renaming
✓ Deleting a Worksheet
✓ Multiple Selections
✓ Enter Without Moving
✓ Word Wrap
✓ XLStartup

"Decision and determination are the engineer and fireman of our train to opportunity and success."

—Burt Lawlor

New Workbook

When you need a new workbook you could go to File/New:

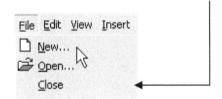

OR

Press **Ctrl** + **N**

"Small differences in ability in key areas can lead to enormous differences in results."

—*Brian Tracy*

Closing a Workbook

There are a couple of ways to close workbooks besides using the **File/Close** command.

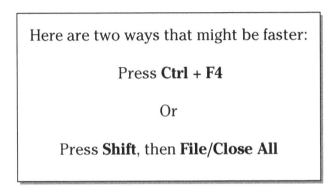

Here are two ways that might be faster:

Press **Ctrl + F4**

Or

Press **Shift**, then **File/Close All**

Note: Holding the **Shift** key down while clicking on the **File** Command dynamically changes the **Close** command to **Close All**.

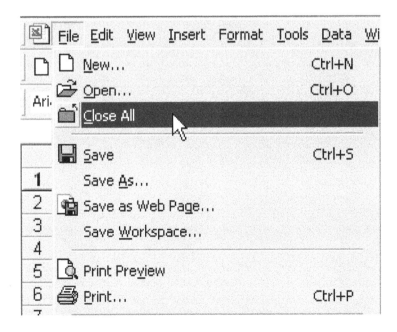

Bonus TIP!

If you want to **Close** Excel
or any application

Press **Alt** + **F4**

Quick New Worksheet

To insert a new worksheet

Press Shift + F11

When you insert a new worksheet, it is positioned prior to the currently selected worksheet. To reposition it click and drag the worksheet tab to the new location.

Note: There is confusion as to the total number of worksheets you can have in a workbook. If you try to enter 256 as the default, you get an error explaining that 255 is the maximum number of sheets in a workbook.

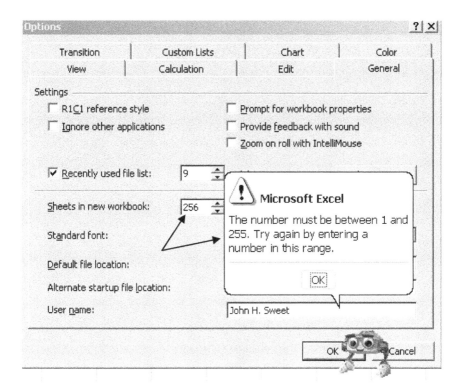

However if you enter 255, the next time you open a new workbook it will have 255 sheets, and you can add 256, 257 etc. until you run out of disk space.

So the **maximum** number of sheets in workbook is limited only by the size of your hard drive!

Easy Sheet Renaming

The easy way to rename a worksheet is to double click on the name, which will select it. Then you can type the new name.

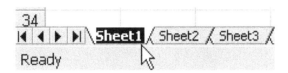

You can use up to 31 characters including numbers and spaces, as well as upper and lower case letters.

"As long as you can start, you are all right. The juice will come."

—*Ernest Hemingway*

Deleting a Worksheet

To delete a worksheet right-click on the worksheet tab

select **Delete**

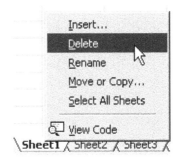

You can select a group of sheets and delete them all at once.

Caution: You might want to save the worksheet before deleting (**Ctrl + S**) because you can't undo deleting a worksheet!

"Knowing is not enough, we must apply.
Willing is not enough, we must do."
                                    —*Johann von Goethe*

Multiple Selections

You can select cells or ranges by holding the **Ctrl** down and clicking the cells you want.

or

You can Press **Shift + F8**, then click, click, click, etc. to select cells and ranges. When you are finished, Press **Esc**.

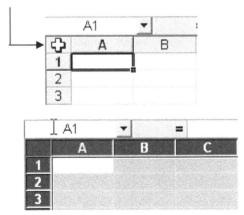

The advantage to using **Shift + F8** is it frees up a hand!

Selecting the whole worksheet is simple. Click on the rectangle at the intersection of the rows and columns.

This will select the entire worksheet. This is handy when your boss doesn't like the font you've used, and you need to change it.

"It is no use saying 'we are doing our best.' You have got to succeed in doing what is necessary."
—*Sir Winston Churchill*

Enter without Moving

There are a couple of ways to enter data without moving from the cell.

Press **Ctrl + Enter**

Or

Click on the check mark

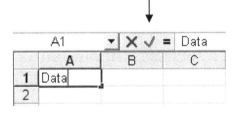

"Striving for success without hard work is like trying to harvest where you haven't planted."

—*David Bly*

Word Wrap

When you want to keep what you are typing in the same cell use Word Wrap.

Here we have text in cell A1:

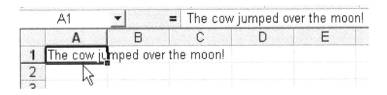

Applying Word Wrap:

Select **Format/Cells/Alignment** tab
Select **Wrap test**
Select **OK**

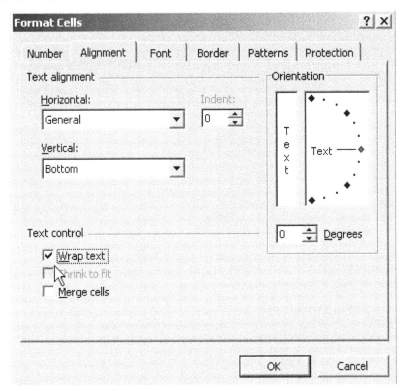

Now your data is in one cell.

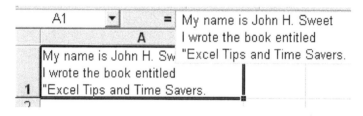

A variation is to move to the next line in a cell as you are entering data. In this case you substitute **ALT** + **Enter** for **Enter**. This allows you to enter data in a single cell and decide where you break the data.

XLStart

When you want to have Microsoft© Excel to open a specific file every time you open the application, simply move or copy the file to the XLStart folder.

C:\Program Files\Microsoft Office\Office\XLStart

Bonus TIP!

If you want all of your new sheets to have a certain look you can change the defaults.

1. Press **Shift + F11** or Select **File/New/Blank Document/OK**
2. Press **Ctrl + A** to select all sells or click rectangle where the row and column identifiers meet.

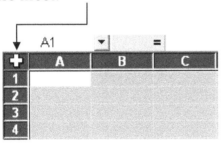

3. Press **Ctrl + 1** or Select **Formal/Cells**
4. Make any formatting changes you want.
5. Press **F12** or Select **File/Save As**
6. Change the **Save as Type** to **Template (*.xlt)**
7. Name the template anything you like.
8. **Save** the new template in the **XLStart** folder.

"The key to success is for you to make a habit throughout your life of doing the things you fear."
—*Brian Tracey*

7
Chart Tips

✓ Quick Add
✓ Default Chart
✓ Two Chart Types
✓ Printing Embedded Charts
✓ 3-D Series
✓ Embedding the Data Labels
✓ Picture Charts

"What we see depends mainly on what we look for."

—*John Lubbock*

Quick Add

Chart the first and the fourth quarters.

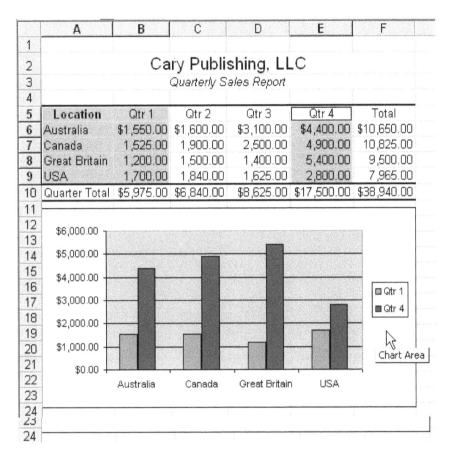

Here is a quick way to add another quarter of information.

1. Select the Qtr 3 data: cells D6 through D9.
2. Position the mouse pointer on the perimeter of the selection until you get the left pointing arrow.
3. Drag the data onto the chart.

Note: When you drag the data onto the chart you will see a small + sign attached to the arrow. The + sign means you are copying, the absence of the + sign means you are moving.

Two things happen when you drag the selection onto the chart.

1. You have added Qtr 3 to the Chart.
2. The plot order is now incorrect. Notice we have Qtr 1, Qtr 4 and then Qtr 3.

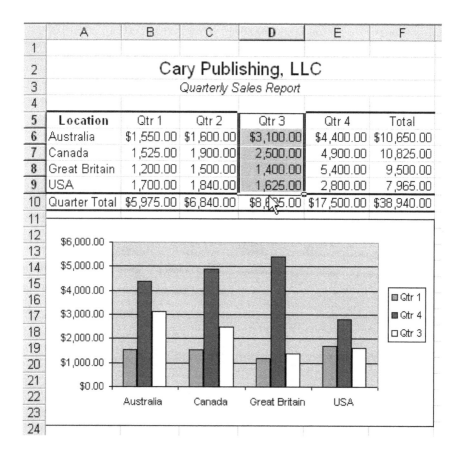

To correct the order:

1. Select the Qtr 3 data series.
2. On the **Format** menu, click **Selected Data Series**.
3. Select the **Series Order** tab.
4. You can put the series in the order you want by selecting the **Move Up** or **Move Down** options.

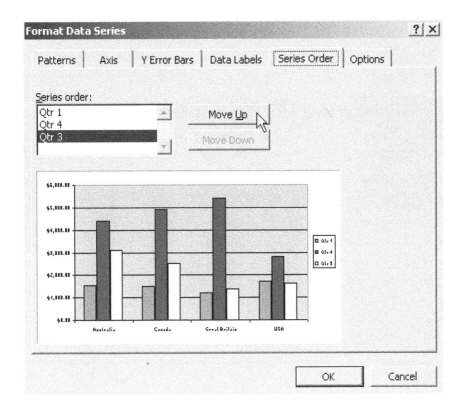

"Nothing is particularly hard if you divide it into small jobs."

—Henry Ford

Default Chart

It is no problem to change the default chart. Here's how.

1. Select the Chart
2. Select **Chart Type** on the **Chart** menu.
3. Select the chart you want from either the **Standard Types** or **Custom Types** tab.
4. Click the **Set As Default Chart** button.

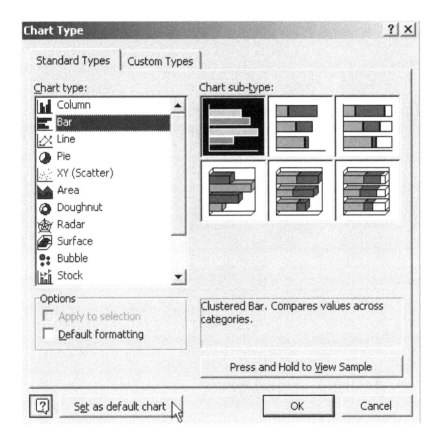

"Patience is the best remedy for every trouble."
—*Marcus Annaeus Seneca*

Two Chart Types

Sometimes you might want to mix chart types. In this example I have combined a Column chart with a Line chart. Here's how:

1. Select the Data Series you want to change to another chart type.
2. Select **Chart Type** from the **Chart** menu.
3. Select the chart type for the selected series.
4. Click **OK.**

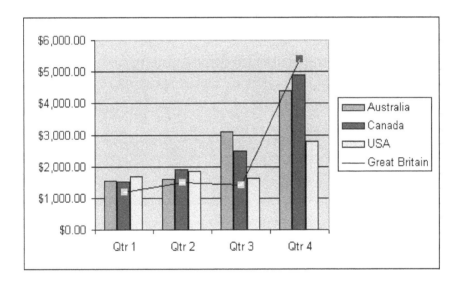

"Success seems to be largely a matter of hanging on after others have let go."

—*William Feather*

Printing Embedded Charts

When you have an embedded chart and your boss wants you to print the chart but not the data, you do not need to move it to a chart sheet to print it by itself.

If you just select **Print Preview** you will see both the data and the chart.

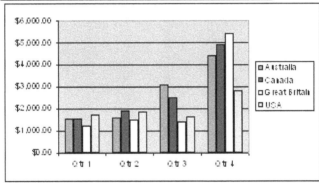

To print just the chart, click on the embedded chart to select it then go to **Print Preview**. Now you see only the chart.

Bonus TIP!

Lying with Statistics.

If you want to de-emphasize the data in a Column chart make it **Landscape** Orientation.

If you want to emphasize the data, make it **Portrait** Orientation.

3-D Series

You can really spice up your bar chart by giving the Data Series a 3-D Look.

1. Right **Click** on one of the Data Points.
2. Select **Format Data Series**.
3. Select the **Patterns Tab/Fill Effects** button.
4. Select the **Gradient tab/Vertical Shading Style**.
5. Select the top left **Variant**.
6. Click **OK/OK**

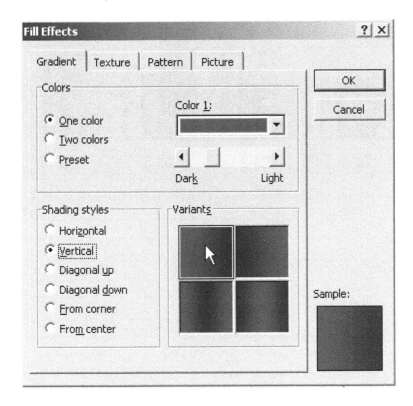

Continue until you have made all of the different Data Series 3-D.

Your graph will now have a really neat 3-D appearance whether you print in black & white or in color!

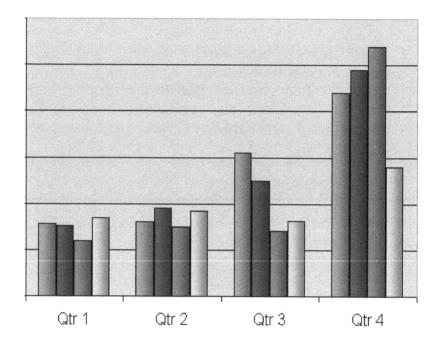

Embedding the Data Labels

With column charts data values can overlap each other in a chart. You might want to use this technique to insert the Data Values into the column.

1. Right click on a data series and select **Format Data Series**.
2. Click on the Data Labels tab and select **Show Value/OK**.

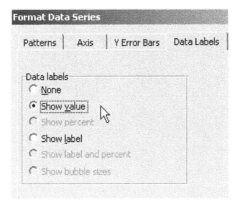

3. Right click on any one of the Values and Select **Format Data Labels**.

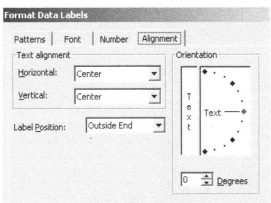

4. Click and Drag the red diamond under **Orientation** down 90°
5. Select **Inside End** from the **Label Position** combination box.
6. Click **OK**

Now the values are inserted into the columns! Neat!

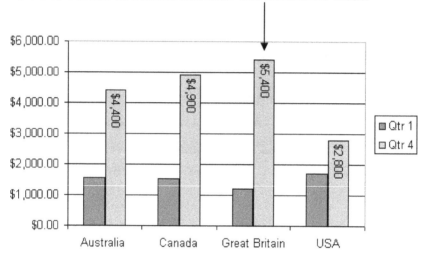

Picture Charts

You might want to use a picture or graphic for your column. This can give a really impressive look to your chart.

1. Right click on your data series and select **Format Data Series.**
2. Click on the **Fill Effects** button.
3. Click on the **Picture** Tab and click on **Select Picture**.
4. Locate the picture file you want to use and Click **Insert**.

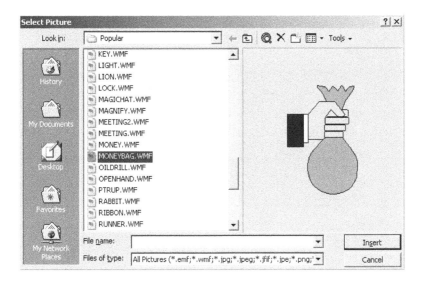

5. Now choose **Stack** in the Format option of the **Fill Effects** dialog box.

This is the **Fill Effects** box with the correct selections.

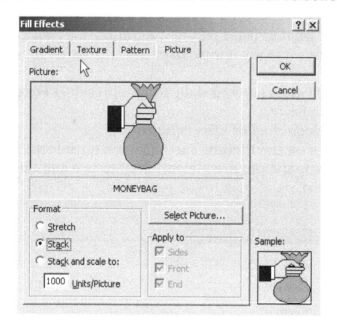

This shows the finished chart!

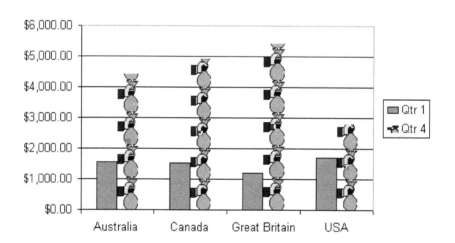

Data Table

Include worksheet detail on your **Chart Sheet**.

Here is the worksheet data for this example.

Cary Publishing, LLC					
Quarterly Sales Report					
Location	Qtr 1	Qtr 2	Qtr 3	Qtr 4	Total
Australia	$1,550.00	$1,600.00	$3,100.00	$4,400.00	$10,650.00
Canada	1,525.00	1,900.00	2,500.00	4,900.00	10,825.00
Great Britain	1,200.00	1,500.00	1,400.00	5,400.00	9,500.00
USA	1,700.00	1,840.00	1,625.00	2,800.00	7,965.00
Quarter Total	$5,975.00	$6,840.00	$8,625.00	$17,500.00	$38,940.00

1. Select your chart sheet tab.
2. Click the **Data Table** button on the Chart Toolbar.
   Or
3. Select **Chart/Chart Options/Data Table** tab and enable the **Show data table** option and click **OK**.

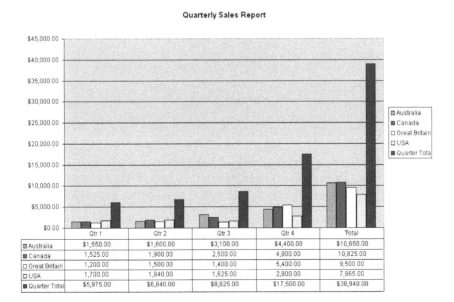

"The difference between truth and fiction: fiction has to make sense."

—*Mark Twain*

8
Graphics

✓ Straight Line
✓ Watch your Fill
✓ Grouping
✓ Graphical Hyperlinks

"There are risks and costs to a program of action. But they are far less than the long-range risks and costs of comfortable inaction"

—*John F. Kennedy*

Straight Line

One thing that seems to drive some people crazy is trying to draw a straight line. The <u>trick</u> to drawing a straight line is:

Holding the **Shift** key down when you draw it!

1. Bring up the Drawing tool bar.
2. Click on the **Line** tool.

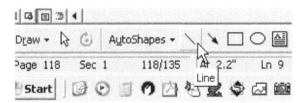

3. Hold down the **Shift** Key and draw the line.

Bonus TIP!

Circles and Squares

To convert an Oval to a Circle
Or
A Rectangle to a Square

Hold the **Shift** key down when you draw it!

"Courage is rightly considered the foremost of the virtues, for upon it all others depend."

—*Winston Churchill*

Watch your Fill

When you draw an object you will by default get the object filled with a color. When you try to make an oval to draw attention to a cell you can't see through the oval.

	A	B	C	D	E	F
1						
2		Cary Publishing, LLC				
3		Quarterly Sales Report				
4						
5	Location	Qtr 1	Qtr 2	Qtr 3	Qtr 4	Total
6	Australia	$1,550.00	$1,600.00	$3,100.00	$4,400.00	$10,650.00
7	Canada	1,525.00	1,900.00	2,500.00	4,900.00	
8	Great Britain	1,200.00	1,500.00	1,400.00	5,400.00	9,500.00
9	USA	1,700.00	1,840.00	1,625.00	2,800.00	7,965.00
10	Quarter Total	$5,975.00	$6,840.00	$8,625.00	$17,500.00	$38,940.00
11						

That is because the default is White Fill.

1. Select the Oval.
2. Double click on the border of the Oval.
3. Change the **Fill Color** to **No Fill**

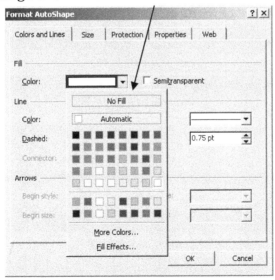

"The secret of success is constancy of purpose."
—*Benjamin Disraeli*

Grouping

When you have two or more objects you want to make into one object, use the Group command. To **Group** the objects

1. Select the objects using the **Shift** key.
2. Right Click on either of the objects.
3. Select **Grouping/Group**

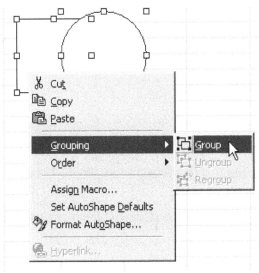

Now you have:

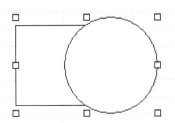

<hr>

Bonus Tip

If you are having a trouble aligning objects or charts on a worksheet, try holding the ALT key down while dragging. The objects frame will snap to cell!

"...the value of expertise must be measured by its impact, not by the time required to dispense it."
—*Dan S. Kennedy*
"How to Succeed in Business
by Breaking All the Rules"

Graphical Hyperlinks

You may want to add a hyperlink to a graphic on your worksheet.

1. Display the Drawing toolbar.
2. Select an **AutoShape.**
3. Format the **AutoShape** and enter any text you want.
4. Select the **AutoShape** and press **CTRL** + K.
5. Enter the path of the web page or worksheet/workbook you want to link to.
6. Click **OK** to create a working hyperlink that's activated when a user clicks on the AutoShape.

Cary Publishing, LLC
Quarterly Sales Report

Location	Qtr 1	Qtr 2	Qtr 3	Qtr 4	Total
Australia	$1,550.00	$1,600.00	$3,100.00	$4,400.00	$10,650.00
Canada	1,525.00	1,900.00	2,500.00	4,900.00	10,825.00
Great Britain	1,200.00	1,500.00	1,400.00	5,400.00	9,500.00
USA	1,700.00	1,840.00	1,625.00	2,800.00	7,965.00
Quarter Total	$5,975.00	$6,840.00	$8,625.00	$17,500.00	$38,940.00

What does Microsoft Think?

http://www.microsoft.com/

Notice that the *callout* is linked to http://www.microsoft.com.

"My success just evolved from working hard at the business at hand each day."

—*Johnny Carson*

9
Formatting

- ✓ Shadow effects
- ✓ Format Painter
- ✓ Styles
- ✓ AutoShape
- ✓ Underline Tool
- ✓ Stripes

"Nothing is a waste of time if you use the experience wisely."

—*Auguste Rodin*

Shadow Effects

One way to differentiate data is to use Shadow Effects.

1. Select the range you want to highlight.
2. Click the Drawing Toolbar's Shadow tool and select **Shadow Style 14**.

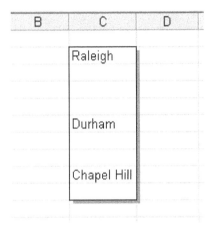

3. Now select the blank cells below the labels one range at a time and apply **Shadow Style 14**.

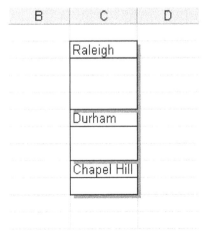

4. Now you might make the columns wider and the
    title rows taller. Try centering the labels to cap off
    the look.

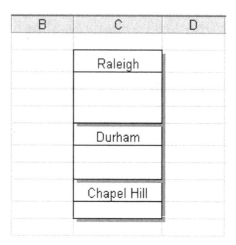

Format Painter

This is a really neat tool. It is a very fast way to copy Formatting from one cell or object to another.

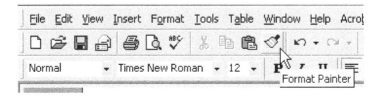

You use it by:

1. Select the cell or object that already has the formatting you want to copy.
2. Click on the **Format Painter** tool on the tool bar.
3. Then **Click** on the cell or object where you want that formatting.

Note: If you want to apply the formatting to more than one cell or object, then double click the **Format Painter** tool. The functionality is then kept on the mouse pointer until you are finished copying. Then you can either click again of the **Format Painter** tool to turn it off, or press **Exc** on the keyboard.

Caution: If you use the Format Painter to copy the same formatting too many times, it makes changing the formatting difficult. If you use the same formatting a large number of times in your document, I suggest using **Styles** rather than **Format Painter**.

"Laboring toward distant aims sets the mind in a higher key, and puts us at our best.

—*C.H. Parkhurst*

Styles

A Style is a collection of formatting that has been saved and can be applied to cells and ranges.

Note: The importance of styles is that once they have been applied to a number of cells, and you change the style, all of the occurrences of the style will change! This is very powerful stuff!

1. Format a cell.
2. Select that cell.
3. Press **Alt + '** (apostrophe) or Select **Format/Style.**

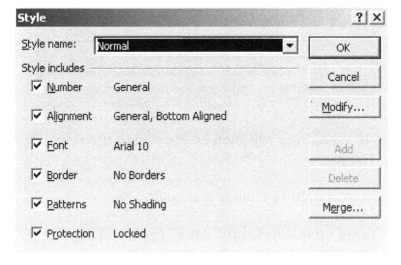

4. Type a **Style** name up to 255 characters.
5. Press **Enter**.

When you want to apply the Style:

1. Select a cell or range.
2. Select **Format/Style** from the Menu bar.
3. Click on the Style Name Combination box to select the Style you want.

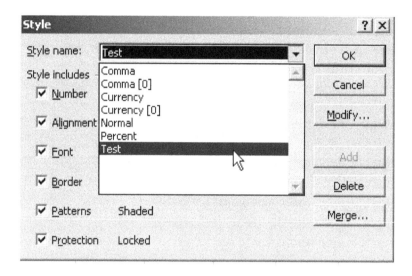

The Style formatting will then be applied to the selected cell or range.

Notice: If you want to change a specific Style.

1. Bring up the Style box: **Alt** + ' (apostrophe).
2. Select the style you want to modify.
3. Click the Modify button.

Any changes you make to the style will be applied to all of the cells that have that specific Style applied.

Bonus Tip
If you want to repeat a **Style**
select the cell and press F4!

AutoShape

Displaying the results of a formula in an AutoShape.

Start with your worksheet. Now lets use an AutoShape to highlight the value of $38,940.00 in F10.

	A	B	C	D	E	F
1						
2		Cary Publishing, LLC				
3		Quarterly Sales Report				
4						
5	Location	Qtr 1	Qtr 2	Qtr 3	Qtr 4	Total
6	Australia	$1,550.00	$1,600.00	$3,100.00	$4,400.00	$10,650.00
7	Canada	1,525.00	1,900.00	2,500.00	4,900.00	10,825.00
8	Great Britain	1,200.00	1,500.00	1,400.00	5,400.00	9,500.00
9	USA	1,700.00	1,840.00	1,625.00	2,800.00	7,965.00
10	Quarter Total	$5,975.00	$6,840.00	$8,625.00	$17,500.00	$38,940.00

1. Select an AutoShape.

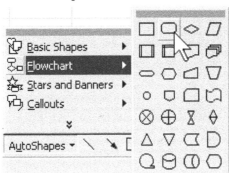

2. Draw the AutoShape in a blank area of your worksheet.
3. Click in the **Formula Bar**.
4. Type an equal sign (=).
5. Click in the cell containing the formula.
6. Click **Enter**.
7. Resize and drag the AutoShape over the cell.

Now you have a great way to highlight the contents of a cell!

	A	B	C	D	E	F
1						
2		Cary Publishing, LLC				
3		Quarterly Sales Report				
4						
5	Location	Qtr 1	Qtr 2	Qtr 3	Qtr 4	Total
6	Australia	$1,550.00	$1,600.00	$3,100.00	$4,400.00	$10,650.00
7	Canada	1,525.00	1,900.00	2,500.00	4,900.00	10,825.00
8	Great Britain	1,200.00	1,500.00	1,400.00	5,400.00	9,500.00
9	USA	1,700.00	1,840.00	1,625.00	2,800.00	965.00
10	Quarter Total	$5,975.00	$6,840.00	$8,625.00	$17,500.0	$38,940.00
11						

Underline Tool

You can underline the contents of a cell.

1. Select **Format/Cells/Format** tab.
2. Select Double from the Underline Dropdown list.
3. Click **OK**.

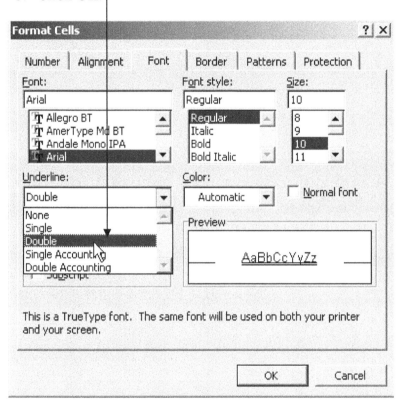

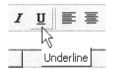

Bonus Tip

You can get the same results by holding the Shift key down while clicking on the Underline tool on the formatting toolbar.

"Most people never run far enough on their first wind to find out they've got a second. Give your dreams all you've got and you'll be amazed at the energy that comes out of you."

—*William James*
1842-1910, Psychologist and Author

Stripes

Sometimes you might want to shade every other line.
Here's a quick tip to do it.

1. Select the first row in your list.

	A	B	C	D	E
1		Beginning			Remaining
2	Month	Principal	Interest	Principal	Principal
3		Balance	Paid	Paid	Amount
4	1	18,000.00	180.00	220.40	17,779.60
5	2	17,779.60	177.80	222.60	17,557.00
6	3	17,557.00	175.57	224.83	17,332.17
7	4	17,332.17	173.32	227.08	17,105.09
8	5	17,105.09	171.05	229.35	16,875.74
9	6	16,875.74	168.76	231.64	16,644.10
10	7	16,644.10	166.44	233.96	16,410.14
11	8	16,410.14	164.10	236.30	16,173.84
12	9	16,173.84	161.74	238.66	15,935.18
13	10	15,935.18	159.35	241.05	15,694.13

2. Apply the shade you want using the fill color tool.

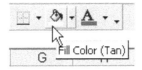

3. Select the first two rows. The first row will have shading and the second one won't.

4. Copy the selection to the clipboard.

5. Select the remaining rows in your list excluding the first two that you copied.

6. Select Edit/Past Special

7. Select Format

8. Click OK

Wow! Now we have every other row shaded!

	A	B	C	D	E
1		Beginning			Remaining
2	Month	Principal	Interest	Principal	Principal
3		Balance	Paid	Paid	Amount
4	1	18,000.00	180.00	220.40	17,779.60
5	2	17,779.60	177.80	222.60	17,557.00
6	3	17,557.00	175.57	224.83	17,332.17
7	4	17,332.17	173.32	227.08	17,105.09
8	5	17,105.09	171.05	229.35	16,875.74
9	6	16,875.74	168.76	231.64	16,644.10
10	7	16,644.10	166.44	233.96	16,410.14
11	8	16,410.14	164.10	236.30	16,173.84
12	9	16,173.84	161.74	238.66	15,935.18
13	10	15,935.18	159.35	241.05	15,694.13

10
Intermediate Stuff

✓ Sorting by Month
✓ Subtotals
✓ Filtering
✓ Mapping
✓ Comments

"Always do whatever you can to keep your superior from making a mistake."

—*Colonel Paul McD. Robinett*
An Army at Dawn by Rick Atkinson

Sorting by Month

The sort command allows you to sort by custom lists. Several custom lists come preprogrammed in Excel. Month is one of them. To sort by month:

1. Click in the row with the month names in it.

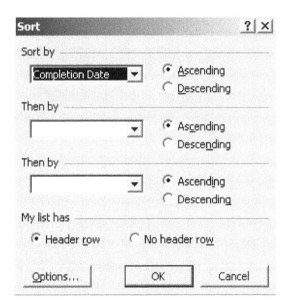

2. Select **Data/Sort**.

3. Click on the **Options** button.

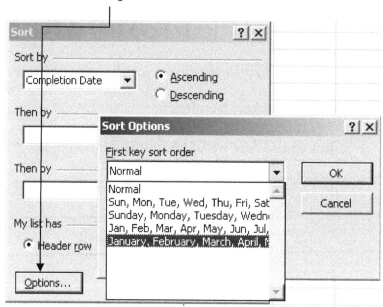

4. Then drop the **First key sort order** combination box down.
5. Select the months of the year.
6. Click **OK**

Now the months are in month order, not alphabetical order!

Subtotals

This is one of my favorite Excel features and it is easy to use.

Caution: You need to **Sort** the column you want to subtotal before attempting to subtotal it.

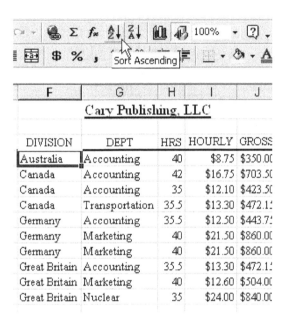

1. Select **Data** on the Menu bar, then **Subtotals...**

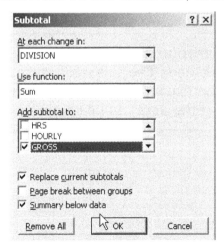

2. Make sure the **At each change in** cell has the column you want to subtotal.

3. Select your Use function field.

4. Click **OK**

1 2 3		A	B	C	D	E
	1		Cary Publishing, LLC			
	2					
	3	DIVISION	DEPT	HRS	HOURLY	GROSS
	4	Australia	Accounting	40	$8.75	$350.00
	5	**Australia Total**				$350.00
	6	Canada	Accounting	42	$16.75	$703.50
	7	Canada	Accounting	35	$12.10	$423.50
	8	Canada	Transportation	35.5	$13.30	$472.15
	9	**Canada Total**				$1,599.15
	10	Germany	Accounting	35.5	$12.50	$443.75
	11	Germany	Marketing	40	$21.50	$860.00
	12	Germany	Marketing	40	$21.50	$860.00
	13	**Germany Total**				$2,163.75
	14	Great Britain	Accounting	35.5	$13.30	$472.15
	15	Great Britain	Marketing	40	$12.60	$504.00
	16	Great Britain	Nuclear	35	$24.00	$840.00
	17	**Great Britain Total**				$1,816.15
	18	**Grand Total**				$5,929.05

> **Notice**: There are outlining symbols on the left side of the worksheet. The plus signs mean that the data can be expanded while the negative signs mean that the data can be compressed.

Filtering

This advanced feature allows you to slice and dice the data many different ways. Great Feature!

Put the insertion point somewhere in the data.
Select **Data/Filter/AutoFilter**

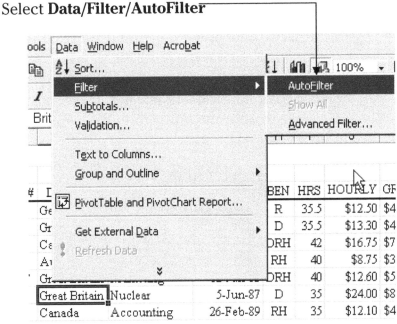

Notice that every column now has an arrow, which allows you to select different items.

D	E	F	G
	Cary Publishing, LLC		
EMl ▾	DIVISIOI ▾	DEPT ▾	HIRE DA: ▾
A29	Germany	Accounting	24-Dec-86
A09	Great Britain	Accounting	5-Jul-85
A58	Canada	Accounting	26-Jul-90
A55	Australia	Accounting	7-Jun-88
AC07	Great Britain	Marketing	12-Jun-83
AS45	Great Britain	Nuclear	5-Jun-87
A19	Canada	Accounting	26-Feb-89
A04	Germany	Marketing	15-Apr-83

Here is how it would look if I wanted to see only the Germany records.

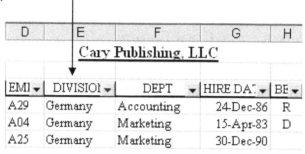

EMI ▾	DIVISIOI ▾	DEPT ▾	HIRE DAT ▾	BE ▾
		Cary Publishing, LLC		
A29	Germany	Accounting	24-Dec-86	R
A04	Germany	Marketing	15-Apr-83	D
A25	Germany	Marketing	30-Dec-90	

You can combine column selections and make custom selections. You reach the custom option by clicking on **Custom...** in the combination box.

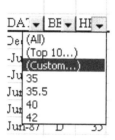

This would allow me to see just the records that have 35 or more hours of work this period.

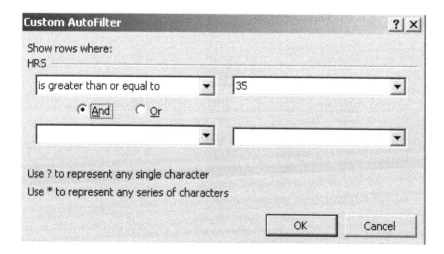

Page 172

Bonus Filtering Tip
Filtering with Automatic Subtotaling

1. Sort on the field you want to subtotal. DIVISION in our example.

2. Place your insertion point in your **List** and select:

   Data/Filter/AutoFilter

Cary Publishing, LLC

DIVISION ▾	DEPT ▾	HIRE DAT▾	BE ▾	HF ▾	HOURL ▾	GROS: ▾
Australia	Accounting	7-Jun-88	RH	40	$8.75	$350.00
Canada	Accounting	26-Jul-90	DRH	42	$16.75	$703.50
Canada	Accounting	26-Feb-89	RH	35	$12.10	$423.50
Canada	Transportation	1-Feb-90	DR	35.5	$13.30	$472.15
Germany	Accounting	24-Dec-86	R	35.5	$12.50	$443.75
Germany	Marketing	15-Apr-83	D	40	$21.50	$860.00
Germany	Marketing	30-Dec-90		40	$21.50	$860.00
Great Britain	Accounting	5-Jul-85	D	35.5	$13.30	$472.15
Great Britain	Marketing	12-Jun-83	DRH	40	$12.60	$504.00
Great Britain	Nuclear	5-Jun-87	D	35	$24.00	$840.00

3. Now filter on a field. Here we use Canada.

Cary Publishing, LLC

DIVISION ▾	DEPT ▾	HIRE DAT▾	BE ▾	HF ▾	HOURL ▾	GROS: ▾
Canada	Accounting	26-Jul-90	DRH	42	$16.75	$703.50
Canada	Accounting	26-Feb-89	RH	35	$12.10	$423.50
Canada	Transportation	1-Feb-90	DR	35.5	$13.30	$472.15

4. Click AutoSum for the Hourly field and you see SUBTOTAL, not SUM. Do the same for any other columns you want to automatically subtotal.

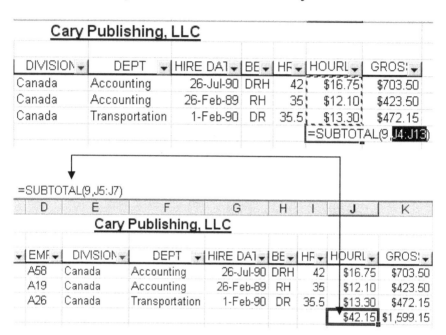

5. **Subtotal** is now dynamic and will reflect the subtotal for any Division you filter.

Cary Publishing, LLC

DIVISION ▾	DEPT ▾	HIRE DAT ▾	BE ▾	HF ▾	HOURL ▾	GROS: ▾
Great Britain	Accounting	5-Jul-85	D	35.5	$13.30	$472.15
Great Britain	Marketing	12-Jun-83	DRH	40	$12.60	$504.00
Great Britain	Nuclear	5-Jun-87	D	35	$24.00	$840.00
				49.9		1816.15

Note: If you enter a SUM function in a column PRIOR to using Auto-Filter the result does NOT change when you filter.

Mapping

You can Map your data in Excel and here are the guidelines.

1. Arrange the information in columns on a worksheet. One column must contain geographic data, such as the names of countries or states.

	A	B
1	State	Total Sales
2	AR	123
3	CA	442
4	CO	5345
5	CT	332
6	DE	2322

2. Select the data you want to map.

   Note: If your worksheet contains additional data for each map feature, such as sales figures for each country, include that data in the cells you select to create the map. If there are headings at the top of your columns, include those heading in the selection.

3. Click on the **Map** icon on your toolbar.

4. Draw a rectangle the size of your map.

You will now see your mapped data!

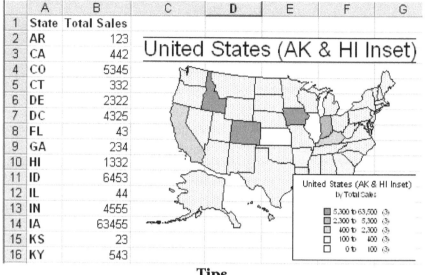

	A	B	C	D	E	F	G
1	State	Total Sales					
2	AR	123					
3	CA	442					
4	CO	5345					
5	CT	332					
6	DE	2322					
7	DC	4325					
8	FL	43					
9	GA	234					
10	HI	1332					
11	ID	6453					
12	IL	44					
13	IN	4555					
14	IA	63455					
15	KS	23					
16	KY	543					

Tips

- **Spelling and abbreviations**   To see a list of standard spellings and abbreviations for map features see the sample workbook Mapstats.xls in the Data folder under the folder where you installed Microsoft Map.

- **Postal codes**   If your data contains numeric postal codes, such as U.S. ZIP Codes, make sure the postal codes are formatted as text or with the ZIP Code number format. Doing so prevents the removal of zeros that might be part of a ZIP Code.

To add the **Map** tool to a toolbar:
- ❖ Show the toolbar you want to add the **Map** tool.
- ❖ Select **Tools/Customize/Commands** tab.
- ❖ In the **Categories** list, click **Insert.**
- ❖ Drag Map from the Commands list to the toolbar.

Comments

Somehow over the years we have stopped documenting what we're doing. Today you can use Comments to document such things as what a complicated formula does.

If you want to insert a comment in a cell, simply right click on the cell and select Insert Comment.

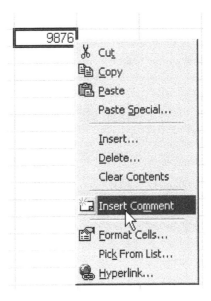

Now you have documented the cell.

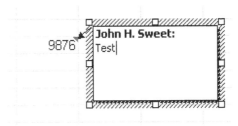

Bonus Tip

Here is how to change the shape of the Comment box.

1. Bring up the Drawing toolbar
2. Select the Comment box
3. Select Draw/Change AutoShape and the shape you want from the AutoShape selections.

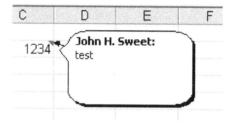

11
File Information

✓ File Properties
✓ Protecting Your Worksheet
✓ Recently Used File List

"Life is like a great grinding wheel. Whether it wears you down or polishes you up depends on what you're made of."

—*Author Unknown*

File Properties

You can find lots of information about Excel files.

1. Select **File/Properties**.

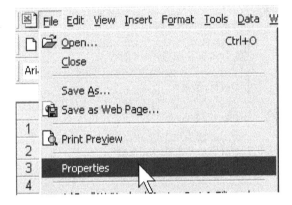

2. Select the **General** tab.

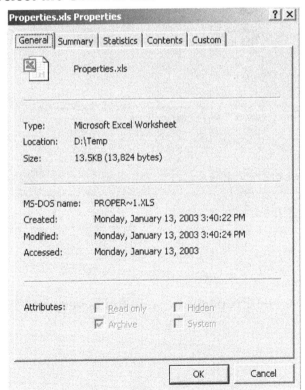

3. Now select the **Summary** tab.

Properties.xls Properties	? X

General | Summary | Statistics | Contents | Custom |

Title: | My Properties File

Subject: | XL Tips & Time Savers Book

Author: | John H. Sweet

Manager: | Holly W. Sweet

Company: | John Sweet & Associates

Category: | Writing

Keywords: | Tips

Comments: | This is for Chapter 11 in my book.

Hyperlink base: | www.CaryPublishing.com

Template:

☐ Save preview picture

| OK | Cancel |

The File/Properties command is very handy!

Protecting Your Worksheet

There are over 16 million cells in a worksheet – the size of an end zone on an American football field! All of the cells are locked by default, so all you have to do is unlock the cells you want to be able to edit.

You can use any standard cell selection to select the cells you want to be able to edit. You usually want to be able to change the cells without formulas in them. Here is a quick way to do that.

1. Select **Edit/Go To**
2. Click the **Special** button
3. Select **Constants** from the **Go To Special** dialog box.
4. Click **OK**.

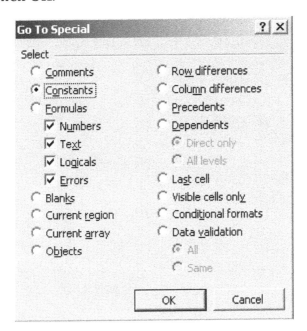

Now all of the cells without formulas are selected.

	A	B	C	D	E	F	G
1							
2							
3		Sales Cary Publishing, LLC					
4							
5		Name	April	May	June	Total	Comm.
6		Dills	18	30	41	$89	$16
7		Sweet	20	12	20	$52	Low Sales
8		Lingle	15	22	25	$62	$11
9		Fox	8	10	21	$39	Low Sales
10		Golay	15	20	21	$56	Low Sales
11		Total					$27.00
12		Note: All Numbers are in thousands.					
13							

Now remove the locks for the selected cells.

1. Select **Format/Cells**
2. Select the **Protection** tab
3. Uncheck **Locked**
4. Click **OK**

And to protect the sheet

5. Select **Tools/Protection/Protect Sheet...**
6. Select **OK**

Now it will be impossible to change the cells that contain formulas.

Recently Used File List

The default number of files available in the File list is 4.

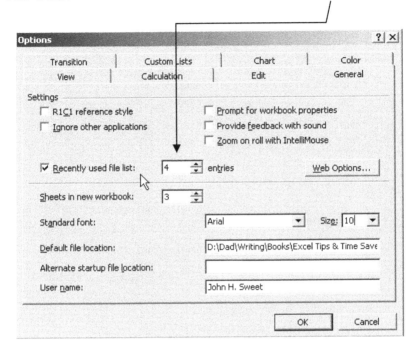

To change this number select **Tools/Options/General Tab**

Then Change the number up to 9 files.

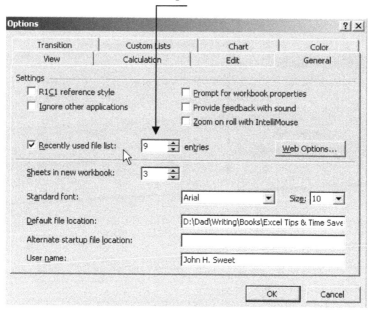

You can now select any of the last 9 files you have used.

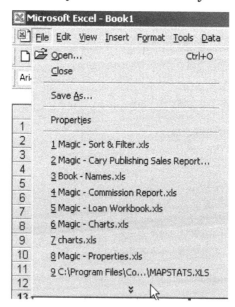

12
Hot Function Tips

- ✓ Instant Function Help
- ✓ Controlling Excel Errors
- ✓ VLOOKUP() made easy
- ✓ TRUNCATE()
- ✓ COUNTIF()

"There are only two ways to live your life. One is as thought nothing is a miracle. The other is as though everything is a miracle."

—*Albert Einstein*

Instant Function Help

When a cell contains a function and you want information about how it works, the quick way is to:

1. **Select** the Cell

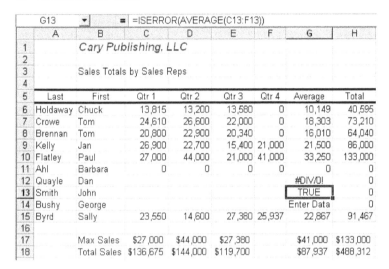

	G13	▼	=	=ISERROR(AVERAGE(C13:F13))				
	A	B	C	D	E	F	G	H
1		*Cary Publishing, LLC*						
2								
3		Sales Totals by Sales Reps						
4								
5	Last	First	Qtr 1	Qtr 2	Qtr 3	Qtr 4	Average	Total
6	Holdaway	Chuck	13,815	13,200	13,580	0	10,149	40,595
7	Crowe	Tom	24,610	26,600	22,000	0	18,303	73,210
8	Brennan	Tom	20,800	22,900	20,340	0	16,010	64,040
9	Kelly	Jan	26,900	22,700	15,400	21,000	21,500	86,000
10	Flatley	Paul	27,000	44,000	21,000	41,000	33,250	133,000
11	Ahl	Barbara	0	0	0	0	0	0
12	Quayle	Dan					#DIV/0!	0
13	Smith	John					TRUE	0
14	Bushy	George					Enter Data	0
15	Byrd	Sally	23,550	14,600	27,380	25,937	22,867	91,467
16								
17		Max Sales	$27,000	$44,000	$27,380		$41,000	$133,000
18		Total Sales	$136,675	$144,000	$119,700		$87,937	$488,312

2. Click on the **Paste Function** tool on the standard toolbar.

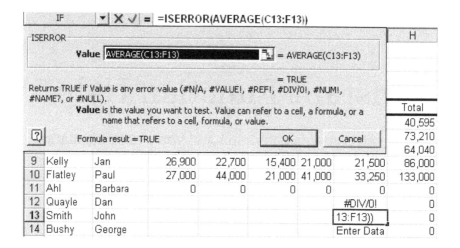

This gives you an onscreen explanation of each argument.

Bonus Tip

If your formula contains nested functions, you can click on any of the functions in the formula on the Formula Bar to change the explanation to the function you choose.

In the above example I will click on the Average function in the Formula Bar and the dialog will now show the Average function.

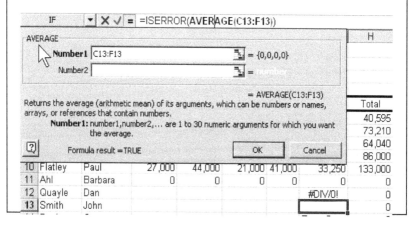

Controlling Excel Errors

Excel can really confuse users with error messages like
#DIV/0!.

 One way to help is to use the **ISERROR()** function, but it substitutes the word TRUE if there is an error. Not much help.

=ISERROR(AVERAGE(C13:F13))

I suggest that you embed the **ISERROR()** function in an **IF()** function and use your own error description.

=IF(ISERROR(AVERAGE(C14:F14)),"Enter Data", AVERAGE(C14:F14))

	G14	▼	■	=IF(ISERROR(AVERAGE(C14:F14)),"Enter Data",AVERAGE(C14:F14))				
	A	B	C	D	E	F	G	H	I
1		Cary Publishing, LLC							
2									
3		Sales Totals by Sales Reps							
4									
5	Last	First	Qtr 1	Qtr 2	Qtr 3	Qtr 4	Average	Total	
6	Holdaway	Chuck	13,815	13,200	13,580	0	10,149	40,595	
7	Crowe	Tom	24,610	26,600	22,000	0	18,303	73,210	
8	Brennan	Tom	20,800	22,900	20,340	0	16,010	64,040	
9	Kelly	Jan	26,900	22,700	15,400	21,000	21,500	86,000	
10	Flatley	Paul	27,000	44,000	21,000	41,000	33,250	133,000	
11	Ahl	Barbara	0	0	0	0	0	0	
12	Quayle	Dan					#DIV/0!	0	
13	Smith	John					TRUE	0	
14	Bushy	George					Enter Data	0	
15	Byrd	Sally	23,550	14,600	27,380	25,937	22,867	91,467	
16									
17		Max Sales	$27,000	$44,000	$27,380		$41,000	$133,000	
18		Total Sales	$136,675	$144,000	$119,700		$87,937	$488,312	

Now if there is an error in calculating the Average, Excel will place "Enter Data" in the cell. If there is no error, Excel will simply calculate Average (C14:F14).

"The key to success is for you to make a habit throughout your life of doing the things you fear."
—*Brian Tracey*

VLOOKUP() Made Easy

This function is a neat way to use a lookup table. You search on the first column until you get a match or fall within a defined range, and then select a value from the same row in a column you indicate in the formula.

Here is the syntax of the VLOOKUP() function:

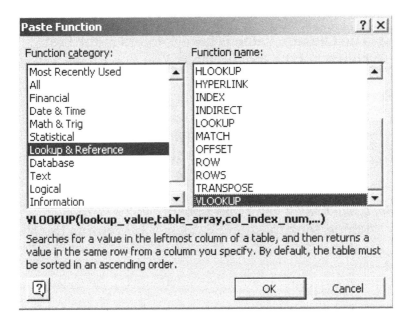

1. **Lookup_value** is the value to be found in the first column of the array. Lookup_value can be a value, a reference, or a text string.

2. **Table_array** is the table of information in which data is looked up.

3. **Col_index_num** is the column number in table_array from which the matching value must be returned.

4. **Range_lookup** is a logical value that specifies whether you want VLOOKUP to find an exact match or an approximate match. If TRUE or omitted, an approximate match is returned. In other words, if an exact match is not found, the next largest value that is less than lookup_value is returned. If FALSE, VLOOKUP will find an exact match. If one is not found, the error value #N/A is returned.

Notes:

❖ The **Lookup_Value** is always found in the first column of the lookup table. You don't have any choice.

❖ If VLOOKUP can't find Lookup_value, and Range_lookup is TRUE, it uses the largest value that is less than or equal to Lookup_value.

❖ If Lookup_value is smaller than the smallest value in the first column of Table_array, VLOOKUP returns the #N/A error value.

❖ If VLOOKUP can't find Lookup_value, and Range_lookup is FALSE, VLOOKUP returns the #N/A value.

❖

Here is an example:

H8		▼		=						
Bonus Table		C	D	E	F	G	H	I	J	K
Comm_Rate										
Quota		Contest: Southwest Region								
3	(All amounts are in thousands of dollars.)									
4						Comm Rate	20%			
5						Quota	50			
6										
7	Name	January	February	March	Total	Commission	Bonus		Sales Contest	
8	Lingle	18	30	23	$71	14.20			Total	Bonus
9	Urmston	20	12	20	$52	10.40			$0	$0
10	Stidham	15	22	25	$62	12.40			$50	$2
11	Hilton	8	10	21	$39	Missed Quota			$60	$4
12	Dills	15	20	21	$56	11.20			$70	$8
13	Total					$48.20				

Bonus_Table refers to the range J9:K12
Comm_Rate refers to H4
Quota refers to H5

We will put the VLOOKUP() function in H8 using the **Paste Function** tool.

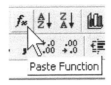

Paste Function

1. We enter F8, the total sales for Lingle, for **Lookup_value**.
2. Then we enter bonus_table in **Table_array**.
3. Finally we put a 2 in **Col_index_num** to indicate which column we want to pull information from. (We leave Range_lookup blank because we do not want to have to have an exact match in our table.)

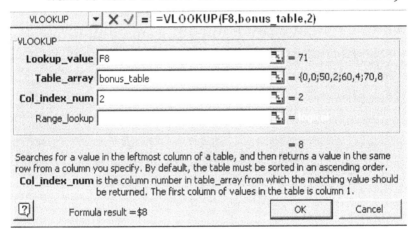

When I **OK** the dialog box and copy the formula down, you have this result.

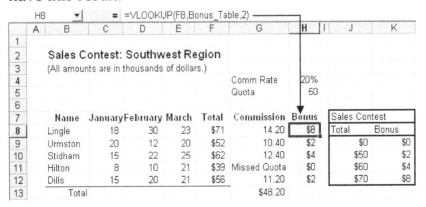

"We pay a heavy price for our fear of failure. It is a powerful obstacle to growth...there is no learning without some difficulty... If you want to keep learning, you must keep on risking failure – all your life."

—John W. Gardner
American educator and public official

TRUNCATE()

Sometimes you <u>don't</u> want to round your numbers, you simply want to cut them off somewhere after the decimal point.

You can use the TRUNC function.

1. Click on the Paste Function tool on the Standard toolbar.

2. Select the **TRUNC** function from the Math & Trig. category.

3. Click **OK**.

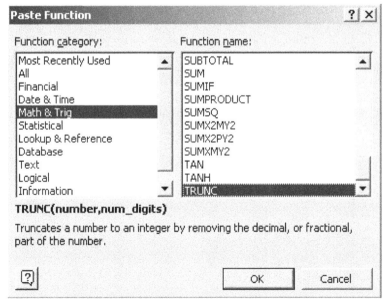

4. Under Number enter either the cell address or a number. In this example. I entered the cell address A1.
5. Enter the number of digits you want after the decimal place. Here I used 3.
6. Click **OK**

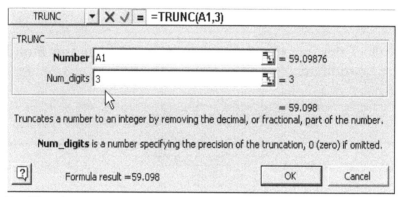

7. The following is the result in B1.

	B1	▼		=	=TRUNC(A1,3)	
	A	B		C	D	
1	59.09876	59.098				
2	66.98765					
3	59.66667					

8. Place the mouse pointer on the fill handle of cell B1 until you get the crosshair and double click.

9. This will copy the formula from B1 through B3, truncating the numbers after three digits in A1 through A3.

	B1	▼		=	=TRUNC(A1,3)	
	A	B		C	D	
1	59.09876	59.098				
2	66.98765	66.987				
3	59.66667	59.666				
4						

COUNTIF()

Sometimes you need to count items conditionally. Lets count the number of employees that have less than 40 hours in our list.

Here I entered the formula:

=COUNTIF(F2:F11,"<40")

Where F2:F11 is the range of cells from which you want to count the employees that worked less than 40 hours.

	F12	▼	=	=COUNTIF(F2:F11,"<40")		
	A	B	C	D	E	F
1	EMP#	DIVISION	DEPT	HIRE DATE	BEN	HRS
2	A29	Germany	Accounting	24-Dec-86	R	35.5
3	A09	Great Britain	Accounting	5-Jul-85	D	35.5
4	A58	Canada	Accounting	26-Jul-90	DRH	42
5	A55	Australia	Accounting	7-Jun-88	RH	40
6	AC07	Great Britain	Marketing	12-Jun-83	DRH	40
7	AS45	Great Britain	Nuclear	5-Jun-87	D	35
8	A19	Canada	Accounting	26-Feb-89	RH	35
9	A04	Germany	Marketing	15-Apr-83	D	40
10	A26	Canada	Transportation	1-Feb-90	DR	35.5
11	A25	Germany	Marketing	30-Dec-90		40
12						5

Note: The <40 is enclosed in quotes. Without the quotes you will get an error.

"Part of the inhumanity of the computer is that, once it is competently programmed and working smoothly, it is completely honest."

—*Isaac Asimov*

13
Auditor's Delight

✓ Auditing Toolbar
✓ Notes
✓ More Auditing Shortcuts

"Day by Day, what you do is who you become."
—*Heraclitus*
?535-475 BC, Greek Philosopher

Auditing Toolbar

Here is how to find where data is coming from and where it is going!

Bring up the Auditing toolbar.

Select Tools/Auditing/Show Auditing Toolbar

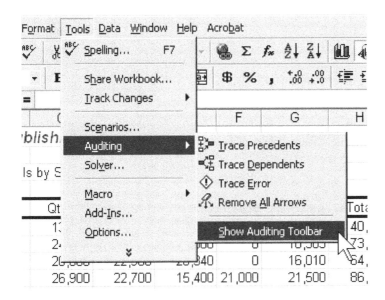

1. The first six tools from the left are:
2. Trace Precedents
3. Remove Precedent Arrows
4. Trace Dependents
5. Remove Dependent Arrows
6. Remove All Arrows
7. Trace Error

This is real auditing POWER!

Here I started in the cell below Qtr 1, then clicked on the Trace Dependents tool two times.

Qtr 1	Qtr 2	Qtr 3	Qtr 4	Average	Total
12,915	13,200	13,500	0	10,149	40,595
24,610	26,600	22,000	0	18,303	73,210
20,800	22,900	20,340	0	16,010	64,040
26,900	22,700	15,400	21,000	21,500	86,000
27,000	44,000	21,000	41,000	33,250	133,000
0	0	0	0	0	0
				#DIV/0!	0
				TRUE	0
				Enter Data	0
23,550	14,600	27,380	25,937	22,867	91,467
$27,000	$44,000	$27,380		$41,000	$133,000
$136,675	$144,000	$119,700		$87,937	$488,312

This works in reverse if you select a cell and use the Trace Precedents tool.

Qtr 1	Qtr 2	Qtr 3	Qtr 4	Average	Total
12,915	13,200	13,500	0	10,149	40,595
24,610	26,600	22,000	0	10,303	73,210
20,800	22,900	20,340	0	16,010	64,040
26,900	22,700	15,400	21,000	21,500	86,000
27,000	44,000	21,000	41,000	33,250	133,000
0	0	0	0	0	0
				#DIV/0!	0
				TRUE	0
				Enter Data	0
23,550	14,600	27,380	25,937	22,867	91,467
$27,000	$44,000	$27,380		$41,000	$133,000
$136,675	$144,000	$119,700		$87,937	$488,312

If you have data coming into a cell from another worksheet or workbook, you will have a dashed arrow leading to a small spreadsheet icon.

	B4	▼	=	=SUM(Indiana:Texas!B4)	
	A	B	C	D	E
1	Summary				
2					
3	Item	QTR 1	QTR 2	QTR 3	QTR 4
4	Hardware	1020	2700	3300	1600
5	Software	1100	1390	2700	1200
6	Equipment	950	1800	2900	900
7	Misc.	900	1331	1400	900
8	Totals:	$3,970	$7,221	$10,300	$4,600
9					
10					

At the bottom left of the icon there is a small triangle. If you double click the triangle you will bring up a dialog box showing the location of all cells from other worksheets and workbooks feeding this cell.

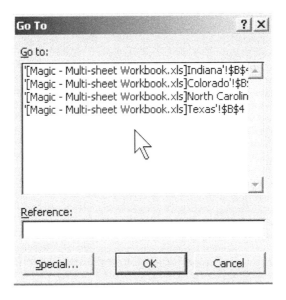

Auditing Notes

❖ Blue arrows show cells in the same worksheet that are dependent on the selected cell. Red arrows show cells that cause errors. If a cell on another worksheet or workbook references the selected cell, a black arrow points from the selected cell to a worksheet icon.

❖ If the dependent cell is in another workbook, that workbook must be open before Excel can trace the dependent cell.

❖ To select the cell at the other end of an arrow, double-click the arrow. To select a dependent cell on another worksheet or workbook, double-click the black arrow and then double-click the reference you want in the **Go to** list.

More Auditing Shortcuts

1. Press **Ctrl** + **[** (Opening Bracket)
   This will highlight all cells a formula references.

2. Press **Ctrl** + **Shift** + **[** (Opening Bracket)
   This highlights cells that feed into cells that a formula references.

3. Press **Ctrl** + **]** (Closing Bracket)
   This selects all formulas a cell feeds into.

4. Press **Ctrl** + **Shift** + **]** (Closing Bracket)
   This selects a dell's direct and indirect dependents.

Bonus Tip!

It might be smart to do a

Ctrl + Shift +] (Closing Bracket)

...before you delete or clear a cell containing
a formula so you can see if it is feeding
another cell!

If this doesn't select any cells, you can safely
delete or clear the formula.

"The minute you settle for less than you deserve, you get even less than you settled for."

—*Maureen Dowd*
New York Times Columnist

Keyboard Shortcuts

Appendix A – Keyboard Shortcuts

Keys for moving and scrolling in a worksheet or workbook

Press	To
Arrow keys	Move one cell up, down, left, or right
CTRL+arrow key	Move to the edge of the current data region
HOME	Move to the beginning of the row
CTRL+HOME	Move to the beginning of the worksheet
CTRL+END	Move to the last cell on the worksheet, which is the cell at the intersection of the rightmost used column and the bottom-most used row (in the lower-right corner), or the cell opposite the home cell, which is typically A1
PAGE DOWN	Move down one screen
PAGE UP	Move up one screen
ALT+PAGE DOWN	Move one screen to the right
ALT+PAGE UP	Move one screen to the left
CTRL+PAGE DOWN	Move to the next sheet in the workbook
CTRL+PAGE UP	Move to the previous sheet in the workbook
CTRL+F6 or CTRL+TAB	Move to the next workbook or window

CTRL+SHIFT+F6 or CTRL+SHIFT+TAB	Move to the previous workbook or window
F6	Move to the next pane in a workbook that has been split
SHIFT+F6	Move to the previous pane in a workbook that has been split
CTRL+BACKSPACE	Scroll to display the active cell
F5	Display the **Go To** dialog box
SHIFT+F5	Display the **Find** dialog box
SHIFT+F4	Repeat the last **Find** action (same as **Find Next**)
TAB	Move between unlocked cells on a protected worksheet

Keys for previewing and printing a document

Note To enlarge the Help window to fill the screen, press ALT+SPACEBAR and then press X. To restore the window to its previous size and location, press ALT+SPACEBAR and then press R. To print this topic, press ALT+O and then press P.

Press	To
CTRL+P or CTRL+SHIFT+F12	Display the **Print** dialog box

Work in print preview

Press	To
Arrow keys	Move around the page when zoomed in
PAGE UP or PAGE DOWN	Move by one page when zoomed out
CTRL+UP ARROW or CTRL+LEFT ARROW	Move to the first page when zoomed out
CTRL+DOWN ARROW or CTRL+RIGHT ARROW	Move to the last page when zoomed out

Keys for working with worksheets, charts, and macros

Note To enlarge the Help window to fill the screen, press ALT+SPACEBAR and then press X. To restore the window to its previous size and location, press ALT+SPACEBAR and then press R. To print this topic, press ALT+O and then press P.

Press	To
SHIFT+F11 or ALT+SHIFT+F1	Insert a new worksheet
F11 or ALT+F1	Create a chart that uses the current range
ALT+F8	Display the **Macro** dialog box
ALT+F11	Display the Visual Basic Editor
CTRL+F11	Insert a Microsoft Excel 4.0 macro sheet
CTRL+PAGE DOWN	Move to the next sheet in the workbook
CTRL+PAGE UP	Move to the previous sheet in the workbook
SHIFT+CTRL+PAGE DOWN	Select the current and next sheet in the workbook
SHIFT+CTRL+PAGE UP	Select the current and previous sheet in the workbook

Keys for entering data on a worksheet

Press	To
ENTER	Complete a cell entry and move down in the selection
ALT+ENTER	Start a new line in the same cell
CTRL+ENTER	Fill the selected cell range with the current entry
SHIFT+ENTER	Complete a cell entry and move up in the selection
TAB	Complete a cell entry and move to the right in the selection
SHIFT+TAB	Complete a cell entry and move to the left in the selection
ESC	Cancel a cell entry
BACKSPACE	Delete the character to the left of the insertion point, or delete the selection
DELETE	Delete the character to the right of the insertion point, or delete the selection
CTRL+DELETE	Delete text to the end of the line
Arrow keys	Move one character up, down, left, or right
HOME	Move to the beginning of the line
F4 or CTRL+Y	Repeat the last action
SHIFT+F2	Edit a cell comment
CTRL+SHIFT+F3	Create names from row and column labels

CTRL+D	Fill down
CTRL+R	Fill to the right
CTRL+F3	Define a name

Keys for formatting data

Note To enlarge the Help window to fill the screen, press ALT+SPACEBAR and then press X. To restore the window to its previous size and location, press ALT+SPACEBAR and then press R. To print this topic, press ALT+O and then press P.

Press	To
ALT+' (apostrophe)	Display the **Style** dialog box
CTRL+1	Display the **Format Cells** dialog box
CTRL+SHIFT+~	Apply the General number format
CTRL+SHIFT+$	Apply the Currency format with two decimal places (negative numbers appear in parentheses)
CTRL+SHIFT+%	Apply the Percentage format with no decimal places
CTRL+SHIFT+^	Apply the Exponential number format with two decimal places
CTRL+SHIFT+#	Apply the Date format with the day, month, and year
CTRL+SHIFT+@	Apply the Time format with the hour and minute, and indicate A.M. or P.M.
CTRL+SHIFT+!	Apply the Number format with two decimal places, thousands separator, and minus sign (–) for negative values
CTRL+SHIFT+&	Apply the outline border
CTRL+SHIFT+_	Remove outline borders

CTRL+B	Apply or remove bold formatting
CTRL+I	Apply or remove italic formatting
CTRL+U	Apply or remove an underline
CTRL+5	Apply or remove strikethrough formatting
CTRL+9	Hide rows
CTRL+SHIFT+((opening parenthesis)	Unhide rows
CTRL+0 (zero)	Hide columns
CTRL+SHIFT+) (closing parenthesis)	Unhide columns

Keys for editing data

Press	To
F2	Edit the active cell and put the insertion point at the end of the line
ESC	Cancel an entry in the cell or formula bar
BACKSPACE	Edit the active cell and then clear it, or delete the preceding character in the active cell as you edit the cell contents
F3	Paste a defined name into a formula
ENTER	Complete a cell entry
CTRL+SHIFT+ENTER	Enter a formula as an array formula
CTRL+A	Display the Formula Palette after you type a function name in a formula
CTRL+SHIFT+A	Insert the argument names and parentheses for a function, after you type a function name in a formula
F7	Display the **Spelling** dialog box

Keys for inserting, deleting, and copying a selection

Press	To
CTRL+C	Copy the selection
CTRL+X	Cut the selection
CTRL+V	Paste the selection
DELETE	Clear the contents of the selection
CTRL+HYPHEN	Delete the selection
CTRL+Z	Undo the last action
CTRL+SHIFT+PLUS SIGN	Insert blank cells

Keys for moving within a selection

Press	To
ENTER	Move from top to bottom within the selection (down), or move in the direction that is selected on the **Edit** tab (**Tools** menu, **Options** command)
SHIFT+ENTER	Move from bottom to top within the selection (up), or move opposite to the direction that is selected on the **Edit** tab (**Tools** menu, **Options** command)
TAB	Move from left to right within the selection, or move down one cell if only one column is selected
SHIFT+TAB	Move from right to left within the selection, or move up one cell if only one column is selected
CTRL+PERIOD	Move clockwise to the next corner of the selection
CTRL+ALT+RIGHT ARROW	Move to the right between nonadjacent selections
CTRL+ALT+LEFT ARROW	Move to the left between nonadjacent selections

Keys for selecting cells, columns, or rows

Press	To
CTRL+SHIFT+* (asterisk)	Select the current region around the active cell (the current region is a data area enclosed by blank rows and blank columns)
SHIFT+arrow key	Extend the selection by one cell
CTRL+SHIFT+arrow key	Extend the selection to the last nonblank cell in the same column or row as the active cell
SHIFT+HOME	Extend the selection to the beginning of the row
CTRL+SHIFT+HOME	Extend the selection to the beginning of the worksheet
CTRL+SHIFT+END	Extend the selection to the last used cell on the worksheet (lower-right corner)
CTRL+SPACEBAR	Select the entire column
SHIFT+SPACEBAR	Select the entire row
CTRL+A	Select the entire worksheet
SHIFT+BACKSPACE	Select only the active cell when multiple cells are selected
SHIFT+PAGE DOWN	Extend the selection down one screen
SHIFT+PAGE UP	Extend the selection up one screen
CTRL+SHIFT+SPACEBAR	With an object selected, select all objects on a sheet

CTRL+6	Alternate between hiding objects, displaying objects, and displaying placeholders for objects
CTRL+7	Show or hide the **Standard** toolbar
F8	Turn on extending a selection by using the arrow keys
SHIFT+F8	Add another range of cells to the selection; or use the arrow keys to move to the start of the range you want to add, and then press F8 and the arrow keys to select the next range
SCROLL LOCK, SHIFT+HOME	Extend the selection to the cell in the upper-left corner of the window
SCROLL LOCK, SHIFT+END	Extend the selection to the cell in the lower-right corner of the window

Keys for selecting cells that have special characteristics

Press	To
CTRL+SHIFT+* (asterisk)	Select the current region around the active cell (the current region is a data area enclosed by blank rows and blank columns)
CTRL+/	Select the current array, which is the array that the active cell belongs to
CTRL+SHIFT+O (the letter O)	Select all cells with comments
CTRL+\	Select cells in a row that don't match the value in the active cell in that row. You must select the row starting with the active cell.
CTRL+SHIFT+		Select cells in a column that don't match the value in the active cell in that column. You must select the column starting with the active cell.
CTRL+[(opening bracket)	Select only cells that are directly referred to by formulas in the selection
CTRL+SHIFT+{ (opening brace)	Select all cells that are directly or indirectly referred to by formulas in the selection
CTRL+] (closing bracket)	Select only cells with formulas that refer directly to the active cell
CTRL+SHIFT+} (closing brace)	Select all cells with formulas that refer directly or indirectly to the active cell

Keys for using AutoFilter

Press	To
Arrow keys to select the cell that contains the column label, and then press ALT+DOWN ARROW	Display the AutoFilter list for the current column
DOWN ARROW	Select the next item in the AutoFilter list
UP ARROW	Select the previous item in the AutoFilter list
ALT+UP ARROW	Close the AutoFilter list for the current column
HOME	Select the first item (**All**) in the AutoFilter list
END	Select the last item in the AutoFilter list
ENTER	Filter the list by using the selected item in the AutoFilter list

Keys for outlining data

Press	To
ALT+SHIFT+RIGHT ARROW	Group rows or columns
ALT+SHIFT+LEFT ARROW	Ungroup rows or columns
CTRL+8	Display or hide outline symbols
CTRL+9	Hide selected rows
CTRL+SHIFT+((opening parenthesis)	Unhide selected rows
CTRL+0 (zero)	Hide selected columns
CTRL+SHIFT+) (closing parenthesis)	Unhide selected columns

Keys for sending e-mail messages

To use keys to send e-mail messages, you must configure Microsoft Outlook as your default e-mail program. If Outlook Express is your default e-mail program, you cannot use most of these keys to send e-mail messages.

Press	To
SHIFT+TAB	Move to the e-mail message header. Cell A1 must be the active cell when you press these keys.
ALT+S	Send the active spreadsheet as an e-mail message
CTRL+SHIFT+B	Open the Address Book
ALT+K	Check the names in the **To**, **Cc**, and **Bcc** boxes against the Address Book
ALT+PERIOD	Open the Address Book in the **To** box
ALT+C	Open the Address Book in the **Cc** box
ALT+B	Open the Address Book in the **Bcc** box
ALT+J	Go to the **Subject** box
ALT+P	Open the Outlook **Message Options** dialog box (**View** menu, **Options** command in a message)
CTRL+SHIFT+G	Create a message flag

Print a list of shortcut keys

1. If the **Contents** tab isn't visible, press ALT+C to display it.

2. Select the heading **Shortcut Keys** or **Using Shortcut Keys**, press ALT+O, and then press P.

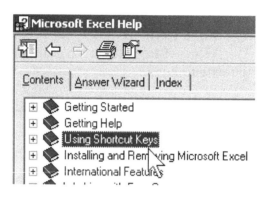

3. Click **Print the selected heading and all subtopics**.

4. Select the printing options you want.

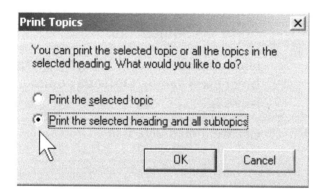

Glossary

Appendix B – Glossary

This is a link to the Microsoft® Glossary:

http://support.microsoft.com/default.aspx?scid=/support/glossary/default.asp

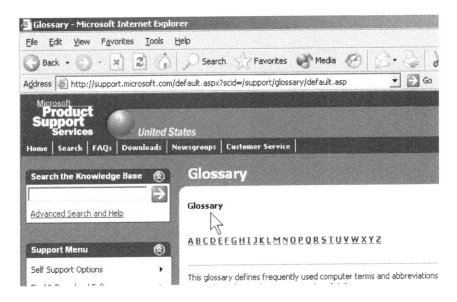

File Extensions

Appendix C – File Extensions

Here are your common Microsoft® Excel extensions.

	File name extension
Microsoft Excel Workbook (Microsoft Excel 97-2000)	.xls
Template (Microsoft Excel 97-2000)	.xlt
Workspace (Microsoft Excel 97-2000)	.xlw
Microsoft Excel 97-2000 & 5.0/95 Workbook	.xls
Microsoft Excel 5.0/95 Workbook	.xls
Microsoft Excel version 4.0 workbook (saves only worksheets, chart sheets, and macro sheets)	.xlw

"Outstanding people have one thing in common: an absolute sense of mission."

—*Zig Ziglar*

Index

"The most important thing about getting somewhere is starting right where you are."

—*Bruce Barton*

Book Order Information

You may order this book

Excel Tips and Time Savers

1. From your local bookstore
   ISBN 1-55369-129-6

   or

2. From Trafford Publishing at this web site

   www.trafford.com/robots/01-0531.html

For information regarding special discounts for bulk purchases, please contact Cary Publishing, LLC at info@carypublishing.com or 919-460-1018.

If you have a tip you think should be in the next revision of this book, please send your Name, E-mail address and the tip to the author:

John H. Sweet
at
jhsweet@nc.rr.com

Thanks,

John H. Sweet

"…you need to be 'at bat' if you ever expect to get a hit, and it's even more important to step back up to the plate after you strike out…"

–*Zig Ziglar*

Book Order Information

You may order this book

Excel Tips and Time Savers

1. From your local bookstore
   ISBN 1-55369-129-6

   or

2. From Trafford Publishing at this web site

   www.trafford.com/robots/01-0531.html

For information regarding special discounts for bulk purchases, please contact Cary Publishing, LLC at info@carypublishing.com or 919-460-1018.

If you have a tip you think should be in the next revision of this book, please send your Name, E-mail address and the tip to the author:

John H. Sweet
at
jhsweet@nc.rr.com

Thanks,

John H. Sweet

www.ingramcontent.com/pod-product-compliance
Lightning Source LLC
Chambersburg PA
CBHW051230050326
40689CB00007B/872